CONVERSATIONS WITH

GOD

• an uncommon dialogue •

CONVERSATIONS WITH

GOD

• an uncommon dialogue •

LIVING IN THE WORLD WITH HONESTY, COURAGE, AND LOVE

NEALE DONALD WALSCH

Expanded Anniversary Edition of
Conversations with God, Book 2

HAMPTON ROADS
PUBLISHING COMPANY, INC.

Cover design by Frame25 Productions
Cover art by Digitalife, c/o Shutterstock

Hampton Roads Publishing Company, Inc.
1125 Stoney Ridge Road
Charlottesville, VA 22902

434-296-2772
fax: 434-296-5096
e-mail: hrpc@hrpub.com
www.hrpub.com

If you are unable to order this book from your local
bookseller, you may order directly from the publisher.
Call 1-800-766-8009, toll-free.

ISBN 978-1-57174-570-5
10 9 8 7 6 5 4 3 2 1
Printed on acid-free paper in Canada

for

Samantha
Tara-Jenelle
Nicholas
Travis
Karus
Tristan
Devon
Dustin
Dylan

*You have gifted me far more
than I ever gifted you.
I have not been the father I had hoped to be.
But wait. We are not through with each other.
This is a work in progress.*

Acknowledgments

Always I want to place at the top of my list of acknowledgments That Which Is All Things, and which is the Source of all things, including this book. Some of you choose to call that God, as do I, yet it matters not what name you give The Source. It was, is, and always will be The Source Forever, and even forever more.

Second, I want to acknowledge that I had wonderful parents, through whom God's sourcing of life itself, and so many of my life's most important rememberings, flowed. Taken together, my Mom and Dad were a terrific team. Not everybody who looked on from the sidelines may have agreed, but the two of them were very clear about that. They called each other "Pest" and "Poison." Mom said Dad was a "pest," and Dad said Mom was a "poison" he could not resist.

My mother, Anne, was an extraordinary person; a woman of endless compassion, of deep understanding, of quiet and unending forgiveness, of seemingly limitless giving, of ongoing patience, of soft wisdom, and of an abiding faith in God so strong that, moments before her death, the new, young priest who had administered to her the final rites of the Roman Catholic Church (and who was clearly nervous) came to me from her bedside trembling with admiration. "My God," he whispered, "she was comforting me."

It is the highest tribute to Mom to say that I wasn't surprised by that.

My father, Alex, had few of the graces of gentler beings. He was blustery, gruff, he could be embarrassingly abrasive, and there are those who say he was often cruel, particularly to my mother. I am not willing to judge him for that (or anything else). My mother refused to judge or condemn him (quite to the contrary, praising him even with her last words), and I cannot imagine how it serves me to ignore her clear example by sinking beneath it.

Besides, Dad had a huge pile of enormously positive traits, traits of which my Mother never lost sight. These included an unwavering belief in the indomitability of the human spirit, and a deep clarity that conditions which needed to be changed were not changed by complaining about them, but by leadership. He taught me that I could do anything I set my mind to. He was a man upon whom his wife and family could, and did, depend until the very end. He was the absolute embodiment of loyalty, of never being a fence-sitter, but always taking a stand, of refusing to take no for an answer from a world which defeated so many others. His mantra in the face of even the most overwhelming odds was, "Ah, there's nothing to it." I used that mantra in every challenging time of my life. It worked every time.

It is the highest tribute to Dad to say that I wasn't surprised by that.

Between the two of them, I felt challenged and called to a place of supreme confidence in myself, and unconditional love for everyone else. What a combo!

In my previous book I acknowledged some other members of my family and circle of friends who've made an enormous contribution to my life—and still do. I want to include now two special people who have come into my life since the first book was written and have made an extraordinary impact on me:

Dr. Leo and Mrs. Letha Bush . . . who have demonstrated to me with their daily lives that in moments of selfless caring for family and loved ones, of concern for friends, of kindness to those in need, of hospitality to all, and of abiding faith and love in and for each other, will be found life's richest rewards. I am instructed by them, and deeply inspired.

Also in this space I wish to acknowledge some of my other teachers, special angels sent to me by God to bring me a particular message which I am now clear it was important for me to hear. Some of them touched me personally, some from a distance, and some from a point on the Matrix so far away that they don't even know (at a conscious level) I exist. Still, their energy has been received here, in my soul. By these beings, in this particular lifetime, I have been gifted and benefited:

Dolly Parton . . . whose music and smile and whole personhood has blessed a nation, and gladdened my heart so often—even when it was broken and I was sure it couldn't be gladdened anymore. Now there's a special magic.

Terry Cole-Whittaker . . . whose wit and wisdom and insight and joy in life and absolute honesty have stood for me as both an example and a measurement since the day I met her. Thousands have been enlarged, enhanced, and enlivened by her.

Neil Diamond . . . who has reached into the depth of his soul for his artistry, and so has reached into the depth of mine, and touched the soul of a generation. His talent, and the emotional generosity with which he has shared it, is monumental.

Thea Alexander . . . who has dared through her writing to shake me awake to the possibility of expressing human affection without limitation, without hurtfulness, without hidden agendas, without bitter jealousies, and without needfulness or expectations. She has reignited in the world the restless spirit of boundless love and our most natural desire for sexual celebration, making it wondrous and beautiful and innocently pure again.

Robert Rimmer . . . who has done exactly the same.

Warren Spahn . . . who taught me that reaching excellence in any area of life means setting the highest standards and refusing to fall back from them; asking the most of oneself, even when accepting the least would hardly be noticed (perhaps, especially then). A sports hero of the first magnitude, a hero on the battlefield under fire, and a life hero who has never wavered in his commitment to excel, no matter how much work it took to do that.

Jimmy Carter . . . who courageously insists on playing international politics by not playing politics, but coming from his heart, and from what he knows under the Highest Law is right. A breath of air so fresh, this stale world has hardly known what to do with it.

Shirley MacLaine . . . who has demonstrated that intellect and entertainment are not mutually exclusive; that we can rise above the base and the banal and the lowest common denominator. She insists that we can talk about larger things as well as small; heavier things as well as light; deeper things as well as shallow. She's struggling to raise the level of our discourse, and so, of our consciousness; to use constructively her enormous influence on the marketplace of ideas.

Oprah Winfrey . . . who is doing exactly the same.

Steven Spielberg . . . who is doing exactly the same.

George Lucas . . . who is doing exactly the same.

Ron Howard . . . who is doing exactly the same.

Hugh Downs . . . who is doing exactly the same.

And Gene Roddenberry . . . whose Spirit can hear this now, and is smiling . . . because he led the way in so much of this; took the gamble; stepped to the edge; went, in truth, where no one had gone before.

These people are treasures, as are we all. Unlike some of us, however, they have chosen to give from their treasury of Self on a massive scale; to put themselves out there in a huge way; to risk all of it, to lose their privacy and throw their personal world into upheaval forever, in order to give of who they truly are. They have not even known whether the gift they had to give would be received. Still, they gave it.

I acknowledge them for that. Thank you all. My life has been made richer by you.

Introduction

I am writing these words in March of 2008 and hoping that some things will have changed in this world from the moment I write these words to the moment (*this* moment) you are reading them.

Isn't it interesting that it is "this moment" both times? Time accordions like that, and I find it fascinating how it does that. Right now it's Now, and as you are reading this it's also Now. It's almost as if no time has passed at all, and yet it has likely been months—possibly even years—between my writing and your reading these words.

What has happened in the interim? I can't possibly know as I write right now, but right now as you read, you *can* know. You can look back over the space between My Now and Your Now—between 11:23 a.m. on March 26, 2008, and whatever day and time it is Right Now in your reality—and you can see what's happened in *my future.*

Interesting way to think about this, isn't it?

But now let's go to an even more interesting place. Let's have the two of us look both forward *and* backward—from the standpoint of my present reality and yours.

As we look forward, let's move past your present moment into what is The Future for both of us.

How do we want that to feel? Any ideas? I hope you have some ideas . . . because, you see, it's the two of us who are going to create that. You and I and a few other folks who are hanging around in the Here and Now are *right this minute* in the process of creating tomorrow.

I am bringing all of this up here, in the preamble to this book, because this book looks forward, too. It looks past my future *and* yours . . . to a day when the ideas of both of us about tomorrow could turn into reality. And it offers some marvelous observations, suggestions, invitations, and ideas about all of that.

This is a very good reason for you to dive into this book right now, because whether you've read it before and just want to get reacquainted with the material, or you are reading it for the first time, I know you'll find it stimulating, thought provoking, inspiring, motivating, and, well, just plain exciting—but only if you see the many marvelous ideas expressed here as real and genuine possibilities. If you see them as "pie in the sky" flights of fancy, the book could leave you feeling frustrated and impatient, hoping and wishing for a life and a future that can never be.

As you surely know (or, gosh, maybe you don't . . .), I began writing this book years ago. What you are holding in your hand is an Anniversary Edition, celebrating the fifteenth anniversary of the day I put down the first words of this manuscript (Easter Sunday, 1993). For this special edition, I have added much very new and very personal commentary. It has been fun for me to create that because it gave me a chance to see how the observations in this text stand up fifteen years later, and also to "catch us up" on where we can all go from here if we are really serious about making the contribution of ideas in *Conversations with God* viable in the world.

As the second book of the original trilogy, this text speaks more toward the specific social and political issues of our day and time than any other entry in the nine-book *CwG* series. It discusses life as it is being lived and as it *could* be lived by the collective called humanity.

There will be no greater challenge in the years immediately ahead than the changing of humanity's cultural story, and I believe that the Anniversary Editions of *CwG—Books 2 and 3* can be extraordinarily useful and truly helpful as a source of insight and ideas as we engage in that process. For this reason, I am very grateful to Hampton Roads Publishing Company for its decision to reissue these books as we move toward the end of the first decade of the New Millennium. They, too, believe in the messages of these conversations. Now if we can get more and more people to explore and embrace these ideas, well, by golly, we might be able to *do something* to create a more wonderful tomorrow—for ourselves, our children and our children's children, and even for The World Entire.

And that is the hope, of course. The hope is that *all* of the books in the *Conversations with God* series will, taken together, offer a Cosmology Possible, a way of looking at the world and of *re-creating* it that will bring an end, at last, to our long global nightmare of conflict, violence, killing, oppression, repression, and depression and produce a beginning, finally, to our ancient dream of harmony, of joyful living, of peace on Earth, and of goodwill to humans everywhere.

Though a decade-and-a-half old, I believe that you will find not a word in this book outdated. In fact, I think you'll find the exact opposite to be true. The book was way ahead of its time when it was written (!) and the words here are more relevant now than ever.

The many thousands who have already read this book and helped to make it a *New York Times* bestseller have called it easily the most controversial of the original *Conversations with God* trilogy. Whereas *CwG—Book 1* looked at individual life and addressed many questions related to it, this book explores the collectively created reality on this planet, touching on global issues and expanding into subjects related to the group experience of the larger human community. Its reissue comes not a moment too soon.

The events of the past several years make it clear that our species has approached the furthest edge of sustainable possibilities. The fact is, we can't keep going on as we have been. We can't. I mean, really. *We can't.*

As I write this, the Internet is filled with reports of a huge chunk of once solid Antarctic ice, seven times the size of Manhattan, suddenly collapsing. As I write this, sectarian violence continues to rage in Iraq, threatening the stability of the region—and of the world. As I write this, a teenager in Sao Paolo is making the news for having confessed to the cold-blooded killing of twelve people. The calmness with which the sixteen-year-old described the murders and how he would have killed three more if he had not been arrested "was scary," a police officer said. "He told us he only killed people who deserved to die, like the young man he shot dead because he wanted to date his sister."

All of these things say something about our society, about our way of living in the world, about the story we have told to ourselves about ourselves . . . and passed on to our young.

No, we can't keep on like this. Our global society is either going to reinvent itself or destroy itself.

This extraordinary book provides some striking possibilities, should we choose to do the former. It offers some daring options. It presents sweeping and belief-shaking visions that could lead the whole of humanity from its dysfunctional past to a glorious and remarkable future.

Now let's take a look at that collective past. . . .

What has it brought us that we are so desperate to hold on to? What widely accepted ideas—religious, political, social, economic, or philosophical—have produced such wonderful outcomes that we cannot imagine living with—that we cannot tolerate—even the slightest expansion or alteration of them?

My own answer is that I can't think of a one. Every idea we've ever had about what it means to be human could use some refitting, it seems to me. Every thought we've ever entertained about the best way to resolve our differences could benefit from some reexamination, it seems to me. Every value we've ever embraced, however sacred, could be enhanced with some honest appraisal and some courageous updating, it seems to me.

(Example: Do we really, really, *really* think that the death penalty is an effective deterrent to violence? Example: Do we really, really, *really* believe that God will not accept us into Heaven if we are wonderful people who just happen to have practiced the "wrong" religion? Example: Do we really, really, *really* hold it to be true that the killing of innocent civilians— or anyone, for that matter—is justified as a means of advancing a social, religious, or political agenda?)

Is it time for us to grow up? Is it time for us to abandon our Neanderthal approach to conflict resolution? Is it time for us to rethink our ideas about who and what God is, about what God wants—and why?

Dare we even talk of these things?

Conversations with God—Book 2 dares to do just that.

I said in the introduction to a previous edition of this book and I'll say it again here: The human race *will* change course, that much I can promise you. The question is not whether that course change will take place, but whether it will come about as a result of coercion or cooperation, of open war or open minds.

It cannot be seriously argued that we do not *need* to seek alternative ways of being and living together. But where to go from here? That is the question. This book offers a basis for beginning discussions. If it is startling in some of its conclusions, perhaps that will serve to shake us loose from our malaise. Indeed, it is the *intention* of this dialogue to do so.

The additional material and the new commentary I have placed here brings me back to the discussion itself with renewed vigor and sparks in me a reignited determination to render the messages in this book accessible to as many people as rapidly as possible.

So then, let the conversations begin—the conversations here and the conversations in your heart and soul, with your family and your friends. Yes, let the conversations begin and let them spread far and wide. For it is conversations, after all, that always have and always will change the world.

Especially when they are . . . conversations with God.

NDW
March 28, 2008
Ashland, Oregon

Forethoughts

CHAPTERS 1—7

I must say that rereading *CwG—Book 2* after all these years has made it very clear to me that this installment in the Conversations with God series offers one of the most cogent, incisive, and brilliant commentaries on the collective experience of humanity that I have ever come across. More importantly, it contains exciting inspirations on how we as sentient beings can get from where we are to where we want to be. Thus, it is not simply an observation about our yesterdays but a road map to our tomorrows. It is about the saving of a species. It is about winning the human race.

I can say all this with complete modesty because I have no experience of having written this book, but rather of simply having asked a slew of questions and then of having had the good judgment to take dictation.

Now, as I move through this text once again years from the moments in which I, as the scribe, took down the responses I was given, I find myself deeply moved and as genuinely impressed as a fresh reader would be by the breadth, the scope, the sweep, and the vision of this astonishing dialogue.

Consider the extraordinary list of topics covered on these pages: Time, Space, Truth, Judgment, Awareness, Consciousness, Fear, Karma, Sex, Money, Life Purpose, Relationships, Heaven, Hell, Enlightenment, Hitler, Right and Wrong, Femininity and Masculinity, the Nature of the Mind, a Worldwide Economic

System, the Global Ecology, a complete new way to do Education, and much, much more—including, of course, continuing commentary on God Himself/Herself/Itself.

The book opens with a discussion of God's Will-Free Will-My Will and the interplay between the three. What is the difference here? *Is* there any difference? It then moves into an exploration of how we can each empower the choices and decisions we make in everyday life—to have them really mean something in our lives and make a difference in our world. Then, advancing quickly, the dialogue invites us to look powerfully at "chance" and "choice," "reaction" and "creation" as contrasting ways of moving through moments of decision in life.

All of this in just the first twenty-six pages. . . .

This text, then, is going to take you for quite a ride. You may find some things here with which you disagree. In fact, *I hope* you will because I have learned that God's intention in bringing us this Dialogue has not been to tell us How It Is, but rather (and far more excitingly), to invite us to decide How We Want It To Be.

Thus, the book becomes not an act of revelation, but an act of creation.

To facilitate the new commentaries that I offer for this Anniversary Edition, I have divided *Book 2,* roughly, into thirds. So I'll now be considering chapters 1–7, then later, chapters 8–15, and finally, chapters 16–20.

This opening third of the text is a fascinating part of the dialogue because it moves rapidly across so many topics. The book does not suffer from piles of preamble, but dives immediately into Stuff That Really Matters. And when you get to the re-cap that opens chapter 3, you realize suddenly how much ground you've covered. Already.

Still, you may feel that you've heard a lot of this . . . a lot of what's been said here . . . before. I want you to be careful because if you're not, you could talk yourself into thinking that this review of Things Already Known has little value. And whoa . . . would *that* be a mistake.

It is true that an observation such as "Life is an ongoing process of creation" is not exactly a showstopper to readers of *Book 1* (or other of the Conversations with God texts), yet what is fascinating about each of these dialogue books is how God's conversations cover old ground in new ways. For instance, the advice here to "stop changing your mind" really hit home with me. This business of staying tightly focused was not emphasized in any of the other CwG writings. So suddenly, "Life is an ongoing process of creation" takes on new meaning, absorbs an important nuance, and says more within its new context than it did within its old.

Also taking on new meaning is human intimacy, thanks to the extraordinary passages in this opening third of the book appearing in chapter 7. Here we are given a breathtaking new definition of human sexuality and a strikingly original description, from a spiritual point of view, of the Body Between Us and of the metaphysics of intimate interactions between people (called Tom and Mary in the book and creating the unforgettable metaphor of "TOMARY").

None of this—nothing even close to this—appears anywhere else in the CwG writings. So while there is in *Book 2* a small amount of circling back over previous observations (necessary to create a context within which the book's forward advancements may be considered and more richly understood), by far the majority of what is presented in this second text breaks new ground.

As a further example, the admonition to "stop trying to figure out what's 'best' for you" was worth the reading of the entire book for me. I also love the place at the beginning of chapter 2 where God carefully and patiently explains that She never, ever, *ever* leaves our presence and that it is we who step away from Him during certain periods of our lives—often at just the "wrong" time!

(I know in my own life it has been not unusual for me to "abandon" God and Godly thoughts when things are going badly and to rejoin God in my bliss when things are going well. It is at moments such as the former that I sometimes have to pinch myself, wake myself up, and tell myself, "Hey, what's wrong with this picture? Isn't now, when things are turning sour, the best time of all to *connect* with God? Wow, what am I doing here?")

So it was nice to reread that passage in chapter 2 where God said to me . . . "I invite you to look at your actions. You've been deeply involved in your physical life. You've paid very little attention to your Soul."

I defended myself, "It's been a challenging period," to which God replied, "Yes, all the more reason to have included your Soul in the process."

Talk about the obvious!

Then God added playfully, "These past months would have all gone much more smoothly with My help. So may I suggest that you don't lose contact?"

Indeed.

I have found it challenging to step into the full living of the message of *Conversations with God*. I'm not going to try to kid you about that.

Now I have to tell you that I thought I'd been doing a pretty good job of at least *trying*—but a reread of this second text in the CwG series has made it clear to me, in retrospect, how far I have yet to go.

Not that I am letting that discourage me. Actually, I am experiencing it as awakening me, inspiring me, motivating me.

The game is far from over, and that's always wonderful news for someone who loves the game.

Some people are a bit put off by my referring to life as a "game," but really, that is often how I experience it. I feel I am being invited to play the Game of the Gods. *And what game is that, exactly?* It is the Endless Game of Self-Creation.

This is different from self-realization, in which we are striving to experience ourselves as Who We Really Are. This is a process of *deciding* Who We Really Are and experiencing *that*. Only a god could do that. A student would do the first, but only a master would attempt the second. The irony here is that in doing the second, the first is accomplished automatically.

I see this as a "game" because it truly can be an experience of playing . . . yet playing with a *purpose*, if you know what I mean. Have you ever seen children earnestly at play? They can be really *earnest* as they play. Watch them sometime. They "make believe" this or "make believe" that, and they do so with utter earnestness. Why? Why are they so serious about their pretending? *Because they want to have the experience of what they are pretending to be, do, and have. They want their pretending to feel real.* And why is this? So they can *know* about that *experientially*.

We are all doing the same thing! We think that because we are adults that we have to stop playing. Actually, the opposite is true. It is when we are adults that we are given the Really Big Toys. So let the games begin!

In truth, *childhood is our training.* We learn how to play. And we've learned so well that now we are playing and we don't even know it. *We think it's real.*

Most of us do, anyway. There are a few who don't, a few who are Aware. Those who are Aware, those who know that we are all playing, have found a way to move through life lightly. They have the wonderful ability to "lighten up" at the most difficult moments. They also have the ability to help others lighten up during the same kinds of challenging moments. In this they demonstrate what Enlightenment is all about.

The opening section of *Book 2* was a doozy for me. These first seven chapters woke me up. Again. Maybe even more so than they did when they first came through me.

As I've already alluded, I find myself even today tempted to abandon God and all that I think that I know about life and how it works when I suddenly find myself facing extremely difficult challenges and conditions. And all that came up for me as I re-read the first part of this book. So I have to admit, I got a little discouraged with myself.

Then my Beloved came home from the video store with a movie that she said she really wanted us to watch together. She'd seen it already and wanted to share it with me. It was all about the life of spiritual teacher Ram Dass.

As you may know, Ram Dass suffered a stroke in the late 1990s. In the film (a marvelous documentary titled *Fierce Grace* that I recommend to everyone!), this kind and gentle man openly admits that "being stroked," as he put it, threw him into a crisis of faith.

In the immediate aftermath of this life-altering experience, he found himself taking a step back from everything he had been teaching and sharing with the world about God and the perfection of day-to-day events in the long journey of the soul. Now here he was in a wheelchair, unable to control half his body and finding it difficult to make his mouth produce the words that danced tantalizingly in the swirl of thoughts in his head.

The movie showed us Ram Dass's movement from suppression to regression to aggression to progression, ultimately catapulting himself past the spiritual place where he had resided before, exceeding his own earlier understandings and teachings. His awareness thus expanded, he valiantly brings us all hope that *whatever* occurs in our lives—even possible debilitation in our senior years (experienced by not all, but many)—holds within it the seeds of spiritual wisdom and grace and the fuel for our further evolution.

This, of course, is the message of *Conversations with God* as well. And so, through his film, one messenger spoke to another—even as I, this messenger, speak to you, now, as the messenger *you* are. For we are *all* messengers, as it turns out, each of us sharing with the world our ideas *about* the world toward the end that our world changes to suit our grandest thoughts in a divine process called The Evolution of a Species.

And that breathtaking, immense, and endless process continues every day—one experience, one message at a time. (Yes, my dear Ram Dass? Yes?)

Another of the messages that I realize, in my afterthoughts on this book, I've had a difficult time with is God's statement to me in chapter 3: "You are perfect, just as you are."

I've heard that before, a hundred times. It has still been difficult for me to grasp. I have to let go of so much stuff in order to hold onto *this*. Letting go, I have found, is not easy. I seem to be clutching things for dear life . . . such as the thought that I am *not* perfect but filled with *im*perfection.

I see things every day that I don't like about myself. I feel things every day that don't even feel good to *me*. Yet I allow myself to feel them anyway. So in a sense, they *must* feel good to me, otherwise I wouldn't keep letting myself feel them. I am thus challenged to ask myself, *Why am I feeling so good about feeling so bad?*

What I have come up with is that feeling bad about myself fulfills my previous notion about myself. It confirms the reality about me that I have been living with so long, having been told about it for so long by others. My religion told me. My parents told me. My family and friends told me. Even the ones who have loved me romantically, who have slept with me in intimacy, told me. *Everyone* has told me about my faults, my problems, my inadequacies, my "bads." How could I believe anything else? How could I feel anything but uncomfortable telling myself (much less hearing from another) that I am wonderful?

Yet here comes God—I mean, GOD HIMSELF, for Heaven's sake—telling me that She thinks I am perfect . . . just . . . exactly . . . as . . . I . . . am.

Aha! I say to myself. It must *not* be "God" saying these things. It must be my own ego *pretending* to be "God"! Yes, that's it! My mind is playing tricks on me. My mind, which refuses to just accept, already, the world's condemnation of me, is running interference for me, protecting me from The Truth of My Badness by laying out a picture of myself as Perfectly Fine Right Now, Just The Way I Am.

What foolishness! What arrogance! What kind of God would tell me that?

And then, just then, I hear a sweet, soft, gentle voice within. "You will deny me three times before the cock crows," it says. And then, after a pause, ". . . unless you don't."

And so this is my challenge. Who to believe: God or Man?

But I did not have time to rest with that question as I moved through this book again. The pace of the dialogue is rapid, and it dares me to "keep up." Soon I was once again revisiting *CwG*'s astonishing message about Hitler, about how (and why) Hitler went to Heaven.

And once more I am challenged at every level of my being. How could this be true? And yet, if it is not true, what hope is there for any of us? Is there not a little bit of Hitler in every one of us? What are we talking about here, then . . . a matter of degree? And what, exactly, is the degree of God's love? Does God love us to a certain degree? And then what? *What happens then?*

Ah, yes, these are all questions I revisited as I re-engaged with this extraordinary *Book 2* dialogue. And I have to tell you, it wasn't easy. This book—in fact, the whole Conversations with God series—is not for sissies.

And just when I was about to indulge in feelings of over-whelm during my rereading, I came across this at the end of chapter 5:

> Do not waste the precious moments of this, your present reality, seeking to unveil all of life's secrets.

Cute. Isn't this God cute?

So go ahead. Read, now, the first seven chapters. If you've read them before, read them again. I promise you, you'll get more out of them than you did the first time around. Or even the second. Or even the third.

I don't care how many times you read this material. Every pass brings you something new.

I promise you.

1

Thank you for coming. Thank you for being here.

You are here by appointment, true; but still, you could have failed to show up. You could have decided not to. You chose instead to be here, at the appointed hour, at the appointed place, for this book to come into your hands. So thank you.

Now if you have done all this subconsciously, without even knowing what you were doing or why, some of this may be a mystery to you, and a little explaining may be in order.

Let's start by causing you to notice that this book has arrived in your life at the right and perfect time. You may not know that now, but when you finish with the experience that is in store for you, you will know it absolutely. Everything happens in perfect order, and the arrival of this book in your life is no exception.

What you have here is that for which you have been looking, that for which you have been yearning, for a very long time. What you have here is your latest—and for some of you perhaps your first—very real contact with God.

This *is* a contact, and it is very real.

God is going to have an actual conversation with you now, through me. I wouldn't have said this a few years ago; I'm saying it now because I've already had such a dialogue and I therefore know that such a thing is possible. Not only is it possible, it is happening all the time. Just as this is happening, right here, right now.

What is important for you to understand is that you, in part, have caused this to happen, just as you have caused this book to be in your hands at this moment. We are all at cause in creating the events of our lives, and we are all co-creators with the One Great Creator in producing each of the circumstances leading up to those events.

My first experience of talking to God on your behalf occurred in 1992–93. I had written an angry letter to God, asking why my life had become such a monument to struggle and failure. In everything from my romantic relationships to my life work to my interactions with my children to my health—*in everything*—I was experiencing nothing but struggle and failure. My letter to God demanded to know why—and what it took to make life work.

To my astonishment, that letter was answered.

How it was answered, and what those answers were, became a book, published in May 1995 under the title *Conversations with God, Book 1*. Perhaps you've heard of it or maybe have even read it. If so, you do not need any further preamble to this book.

If you are not familiar with the first book, I hope you soon will be, because *Book 1* outlines in much greater detail how all of this began and answers many questions about our personal lives—questions about money, love, sex, God, health and sickness, eating, relationships, "right work," and many other aspects of our day-to-day experience—which are not addressed here.

If there is one gift I would ask God to give to the world at this time, it would be the information in *Book 1*. True to form (*"Even before you ask, I will have answered."*), God has already done so.

So I hope that, after reading this book (or maybe even before you finish it), you will choose to read the first. It's all a matter of choice, just as Pure Choice brought you to these words right now. Just as Pure Choice has created every experience you ever had. (A concept that is explained in that first book.)

These first paragraphs of *Book 2* were written in March 1996, to provide a brief introduction to the information which follows. As in *Book 1*, the process by which this information "arrived" was exquisitely simple. On a blank sheet of paper, I would merely write a question—any question . . . usually, the first question that came to my head—and no sooner was the question written than the answer would form in my head, as if Someone were whispering in my ear. I was taking dictation!

With the exception of these few opening lines, all the material in this book was placed on paper between Spring 1993 and a little over one year later. I'd like to present it to you now, just as it came from me and was given to me. . . .

* * *

It is Easter Sunday 1993, and—as instructed—I am here. I am here, pencil in hand, writing pad before me, ready to begin.

I suppose I should tell you God asked me to be here. We had a date. We're to begin—today—*Book 2*, the second in a trilogy which God and I and you are experiencing together.

I have no idea yet what this book is going to say, or even the specific subjects that we'll touch upon. That's because there is no plan for this book in my head. There can't be. I'm not the one deciding what's going to go into it. God is.

On Easter Sunday 1992—one year ago today—God began a dialogue with me. I know that sounds ridiculous, but it's what happened. Not long ago, that dialogue ended. I was given instructions to take a rest . . . but told also that I had a "date" to return to this conversation this day.

You have a date, too. You're keeping it right now. I am clear that this book is being written not only to me, but to you *through* me. Apparently you've been looking for God—and for Word *from* God—for a very long time. So have I.

Today we shall find God together. That is always the best way to find God. Together. We shall never find God apart. I mean that two ways. I mean we shall never find God so long as *we* are apart. For the first step in finding that we are not apart from God is finding that we are not apart from each other, and until we know and realize that all of *us* are One, we cannot know and realize that we and God are One.

God is not apart from us, ever, and we only *think* we are apart from God.

It's a common error. We also think we're apart from each other. And so the fastest way to "find God," I've discovered, is to find each other. To stop hiding out from each other. And, of course, to stop hiding out from ourselves.

The fastest way to stop hiding out is to tell the truth. To everyone. All the time.

Start telling the truth now, and never stop. Begin by telling the truth to yourself about yourself. Then tell the truth to yourself about another. Then tell the truth about yourself to another. Then tell the truth about another to that other. Finally, tell the truth to everyone about everything.

These are the *Five Levels of Truth Telling*. This is the five-fold path to freedom. The truth *shall* set you free.

This book is about truth. Not my truth, God's truth.

Our initial dialogue—God's and mine—was concluded just a month ago. I assume this one will go just like the first. That is, I ask questions and God answers. I guess I'll stop, and ask God right now.

God—is this how it's going to go?

Yes.

I thought so.

Except that in this book I'll bring some subjects up Myself, without you asking. I didn't do much of that in the first book, as you know.

Yes. Why are You adding that twist here?

Because this book is being written at My request. I asked you here—as you've pointed out. The first book was a project you started by yourself.

With the first book you had an agenda. With this book you have no agenda, except to do My Will.

Yes. That's correct.

That, Neale, is a very good place to be. I hope you—and others—will go to that place often.

But I thought Your Will was my will. How can I *not* do Your Will if it's the same as mine?

That is an intricate question—and not a bad place to start; not a bad place at all for us to begin this dialogue.

Let's go back a few paces. I have never said that My Will was your will.

Yes, You have! In the last book, You said to me very clearly: "Your will is My Will."

Indeed—but that is not the same thing.

It's not? You could have fooled me.

When I say "Your will is My Will," that is not the same thing as saying My Will is your will.

If you did My Will all the time, there would be nothing more for you to do to achieve Enlightenment. The process would be over. You would be already there.

One *day* of doing nothing but My Will would bring you Enlightenment. If you had been doing My Will all the years you've been alive, you'd hardly need to be involved in this book right now.

So it's clear you have not been doing My Will. In fact, most of the time you don't even *know* My Will.

I don't?

No, you don't.

Then why don't You tell me what it is?

I do. You just don't listen. And when you do listen, you don't really hear. And when you do hear, you don't believe what you're hearing. And when you do believe what you're hearing, you don't follow instructions anyway.

So to say that My Will is your will is demonstrably inaccurate.

On the other hand, your will *is* My Will. First, because I know it. Second, because I accept it. Third, because I praise it. Fourth, because I love it. Fifth, because I own it and *call it My Own.*

This means *you* have *free* will to do as you wish—and that I *make* your will Mine, through unconditional love.

Now for My Will to be yours, you would have to do the same.

First, you would have to know it. Second, you would have to accept it. Third, you would have to praise it. Fourth, you would have to love it. Finally, you would have to *call it your own.*

In the whole history of your race, only a few of you have ever done this consistently. A handful of others have done it nearly always. Many have done it a great deal. A whole slew of people have done it from time to time. And virtually everyone has done it on rare occasion—although some have never done it at all.

Which category am I in?

Does it matter? Which category do you want to be in *from now on?* Isn't that the pertinent question?

Yes.

And your answer?

I'd like to be in the first category. I'd like to know and do Your Will all the time.

That's laudable, commendable, and probably impossible.

Why?

Because you have far too much growing to do before you can claim that. Yet I tell you this: You *could* claim that, you could move to Godhood, this *instant* if you chose to. Your growth need not take so much time.

Then why *has* it taken so much time?

Indeed. Why has it? What are you waiting for? Surely you don't believe it is I holding you back?

No. I'm clear that I'm holding myself back.

Good. Clarity is the first step to mastery.

I'd like to get to mastery. How can I do that?

Keep reading this book. That's exactly where I'm taking you.

2

I'm not sure I know where this book is going. I'm not sure where to begin.

Let's take time.

How much time do we need to take? It's already taken me *five months* to get from the first chapter to this. I know that people read this and think it's all put down in one even, uninterrupted flow. They don't realize that 20 *weeks* separated the 32nd and 33rd paragraph of this book. They don't understand that sometimes the moments of inspiration are half a *year apart*. How much time do we have to take?

That's not what I meant. I mean, let's take "Time" as our first subject, as a place to begin.

Oh. Okay. But while we're on the subject, why *does* it take months sometimes to complete a simple paragraph? Why are You so long between visits?

My dear and wonderful son, I am not long between "visits." I am never *not* with you. You are simply not always *aware*.

Why? Why am I not aware of You if You're always here?

Because your life gets caught up in other things. Let's face it; you've had a pretty busy five months.

I have. Yes, I have. A lot's been going on.

And you've made these things more important than Me.

That doesn't feel like my truth.

> I invite you to look at your actions. You've been deeply involved in your physical life. You've paid very little attention to your soul.

It's been a challenging period.

> Yes. All the more reason to have included your soul in the process. These past months would have all gone much more smoothly with My help. So may I suggest that you don't lose contact?

I try to stay close, but I seem to get lost—caught up, as You put it—in my own drama. And then, somehow, I don't find time for You. I don't meditate. I don't pray. And I certainly don't write.

> I know. It's an irony of life that when you need our connection the most, you step away from it.

How can I stop doing that?

> Stop doing that.

That's what I just said. But how?

> You stop doing that by stopping doing that.

It's not that simple.

> It is that simple.

I wish it were.

> Then it *really* will be, because what you wish is My command. Remember, My cherished one, your desires are My desires. Your will is My Will.

All right. Okay. Then I wish for this book to be finished by March. It's October now. I wish for no more five-month gaps in the material coming.

So will it be.

Good.

Unless it's not.

Oh, man. Do we have to play these games?

No. But so far that's how you've decided to live your Life. You keep changing your mind. Remember, life is an ongoing process of creation. You are creating your reality every minute. The decision you make today is often not the choice you make tomorrow. Yet here is a secret of all Masters: *keep choosing the same thing.*

Over and over again? Once is not enough?

Over and over until your will is made manifest in your reality.

For some that could take years. For some, months. For others, weeks. For those approaching mastery, days, hours, or even minutes. For *Masters,* creation is *instantaneous.*

You can tell you are on your way to mastery when you see the gap closing between Willing and Experiencing.

You said, "The decision you make today is often not the choice you make tomorrow." So what? Are You saying we should never indulge in a change of mind?

Change your mind all you want. Yet remember that with each change of mind comes a change in the direction of the whole universe.

When you "make up your mind" about something, you set the universe into motion. Forces beyond your ability to comprehend—far more subtle and complex than you could imagine—are engaged in a process, the intricate dynamics of which you are only just now beginning to understand.

These forces and this process are all part of the extraordinary web of interactive energies which comprise the entirety of existence which you call life itself.

They are, in essence, *Me*.

So when I change my mind I'm making it difficult for You, is that it?

Nothing is difficult for Me—but you might be making things very difficult for yourself. Therefore, be of one mind and of single purpose about a thing. And don't take your mind off of it until you have produced it in reality. Keep focused. Stay centered.

This is what is meant by being single-minded. If you choose something, choose it with all your might, with all your heart. Don't be faint-hearted. Keep going! Keep moving toward it. Be determined.

Don't take *no* for an answer.

Exactly.

But what if *no is* the right answer? What if what we want is not for us—not for our own good, not in our best interests? Then you won't give it to us, right?

Wrong. I will "give" you whatever you call forth, whether it's "good" for you or "bad" for you. Have you looked at your life lately?

But I've been taught that we can't always have what we desire—that God won't give it to us if it's not for our highest good.

That's something people tell you when they want you not to be disappointed with a particular outcome.

First of all, let's move back to clarity about our relationship. I don't "give" you anything—you call it forth. *Book 1* explains exactly how you do this, in considerable detail.

Secondly, I don't make a judgment about what you call forth. I don't call a thing "good" or "bad." (You, too, would do well to not do so.)

You are a creative being—made in the image and likeness of God. You may have whatever you choose. But you may not have anything you want. In fact, you'll never get *anything* you want if you want it badly enough.

I know. You explained that in *Book 1* as well. You said that the act of wanting a thing pushes it away from us.

Yes, and do you remember why?

Because thoughts are creative, and the thought of wanting a thing is a statement to the universe—a declaration of a truth—which the universe then produces in my reality.

Precisely! Exactly! You *have* learned. You *do* understand. That's great.

Yes, that's how it works. The moment you say "I want" something, the universe says "Indeed you do" and gives you that precise experience—*the experience of "wanting" it!*

Whatever you put after the word "I" becomes your creative command. The genie in the bottle—which I Am—exists but to obey.

I produce what you call forth! You call forth precisely what you think, feel, and say. It's as simple as that.

So tell me again—why does it take so much time for me to create the reality I choose?

For a number of reasons. Because you do not believe you can have what you choose. Because you do not know *what* to choose. Because you keep trying to figure out what's "best" for you. Because you want guarantees ahead of time that all your choices will be "good." And because you keep changing your mind!

Let me see if I understand. I shouldn't try to figure out what's best for me?

"Best" is a relative term, depending on a hundred variables. That makes choices very difficult. There should be only one consideration when making any decision—Is this a statement of Who I Am? Is this an announcement of Who I Choose to Be?

All of life should be such an announcement. In fact, all of life *is*. You can allow that announcement to be made by *chance* or by *choice*.

A life lived by choice is a life of conscious action. A life lived by chance is a life of unconscious reaction.

Reaction is just that—an action you have taken before. When you "re-act," what you do is assess the incoming data, search your memory bank for the same or nearly the same experience, and *act the way you did before*. This is all the work of the mind, not of your soul.

Your soul would have you search *its* "memory" to see how you might create a truly *genuine experience* of You in the Now Moment. This is the experience of "soul searching" of which you have so often heard, but you have to be literally "out of your mind" to do it.

When you spend your time trying to figure out what's "best" for you, you are doing just that: *spending your time*. Better to *save* your time than to spend it wastefully.

It is a great time-saver to be out of your mind. Decisions are reached quickly, choices are activated rapidly, because your soul creates out of present experience

24

only, without review, analysis, and criticism of past encounters.

Remember this: the soul creates, the mind reacts.

The soul knows in Its wisdom that the experience you are having in This Moment is an experience sent to you by God before you had any conscious awareness of it. This is what is meant by a "pre-sent" experience. It's already on the way to you even as you are seeking it—for even before you ask, I shall have answered you. Every Now Moment is a glorious gift from God. That's why it is called the *present*.

The soul intuitively seeks the perfect circumstance and situation now needed to heal wrong thought and bring you the rightful experience of Who You Really Are.

It is the soul's desire to bring you back to God—to bring you home to Me.

It is the soul's intention to know itself *experientially*—and thus to know Me. For the soul understands that You and I are One, even as the mind denies this truth and the body acts out this denial.

Therefore, in moments of great decision, be out of your mind, and do some soul searching instead.

The soul understands what the mind cannot conceive.

If you spend your time trying to figure out what's "best" for you, your choices will be cautious, your decisions will take forever, and your journey will be launched on a sea of expectations.

If you are not careful, you will *drown* in your expectations.

Whew! That's quite an answer! But how do I listen to my soul? How do I know what I'm hearing?

The soul speaks to you in feelings. Listen to your feelings. Follow your feelings. Honor your feelings.

Why does it seem to me that honoring my feelings is precisely what has caused me to get into trouble in the first place?

Because you have labeled growth "trouble," and standing still "safe."

I tell you this: Your feelings will *never* get you into "trouble," because your feelings are your *truth*.

If you want to live a life where you never follow your feelings, but where every feeling is filtered through the machinery of your Mind, go right ahead. Make your decisions based on your Mind's analysis of the situation. But don't look for joy in such machinations, nor for celebration of Who You Truly Are.

Remember this: True celebration is mindless.

If you listen to your soul you will know what is "best" for you, because what is best for you is what is true for you.

When you act only out of what is true for you, you speed your way down the path. When you *create* an experience based on your "now truth" rather than *react* to an experience based on a "past truth," you produce a "new you."

Why does it take so much time to create the reality you choose? This is why: because you have not been living your truth.

Know the truth, and the truth shall set you free.

Yet once you come to know your truth, don't keep *changing your mind about it.* This is your mind trying to figure out what's "best." Stop it! Get out of your mind. Get back to your *senses!*

That is what is *meant* by "getting back to your senses." It is a returning to how you *feel*, not how you *think*. Your thoughts are just that—thoughts. Mental constructions. "Made up" creations of your mind. But your *feelings*— now *they* are real.

Feelings are the language of the soul. And your soul is your truth.

There. Now does that tie it all together for you?

Does this mean we are to express any feeling—no matter how negative or destructive?

Feelings are neither negative nor destructive. They are simply truths. How you express your truth is what matters.

When you express your truth with love, negative and damaging results rarely occur, and, when they do, it is usually because someone else has chosen to experience your truth in a negative or damaging way. In such a case, there is probably nothing you can do to avoid the outcome.

Certainly, *failing* to express your truth would hardly be appropriate. Yet people do this all the time. So afraid are they to cause or to face possible unpleasantness that they hide their truth altogether.

Remember this: It is not nearly so important how well a message is received as how well it is sent.

You cannot take responsibility for how well another accepts your truth; you can only ensure how well it is communicated. And by how well, I don't mean merely how clearly; I mean how lovingly, how compassionately, how sensitively, how courageously, and how completely.

This leaves no room for half truths, the "brutal truth," or even the "plain truth." It does mean the truth, the whole truth, and nothing but the truth, so help you God.

It's the "so help you God" part that brings in the Godly qualities of love and compassion—for I will help you communicate in this way always, if you will ask Me.

So yes, express what you call your most "negative" feelings, but not destructively.

Failure to express (i.e. push out) negative feelings does not make them go away; it *keeps them in*. Negativity "kept in" harms the body and burdens the soul.

But if another person hears every negative thought you have about that person, it would have to affect the relationship, no matter how lovingly those thoughts were delivered.

I said to express (push out, get rid of) your negative feelings—I did not say how, or to whom.

All negativity need not be shared with the person about whom it is felt. It is only necessary to communicate these feelings to the other when failure to do so would compromise your integrity or cause another to believe an untruth.

Negativity is never a sign of ultimate truth, even if it seems like your truth at the moment. It may arise out of an unhealed part of you. In fact, *always it does.*

That is why it is so important to get these negativities out, to release them. Only by letting go of them—putting them out there, placing them in front of you—can you see them clearly enough to know whether you really believe them.

You have all said things—ugly things—only to discover that, once having been said, they no longer feel "true."

You have all expressed feelings—from fear to anger to rage—only to discover that, once having been expressed, they no longer reveal how you *really* feel.

In this way, feelings can be tricky. Feelings *are* the language of the soul, but you must make sure you are listening to your *true feelings* and not some counterfeit model constructed in your mind.

Oh, man, so now I can't even trust my *feelings.* Great! I thought that was the way to truth! I thought that was what You were *teaching* me.

It *is.* I *am.* But listen, because it is more complex than you now understand. Some feelings are *true feelings*— that is, feelings born in the soul—and some feelings are counterfeit feelings. These are constructed in your mind.

In other words, they are not "feelings" at all—they are *thoughts*. Thoughts *masquerading* as feelings.

These thoughts are based on your previous experience and on the observed experience of others. You see someone grimace when having a tooth pulled, *you* grimace when having *your* tooth pulled. It may not even *hurt*, but you grimace anyway. Your reaction has nothing to do with reality, only how you *perceive* reality, based on the experience of others or on something that's happened to *you* in the *past*.

The greatest challenge as human beings is to Be Here Now, to stop making things up! Stop creating thoughts about a pre-sent moment (a moment you "sent" yourself *before* you had a thought about it). Be *in the moment*. Remember, you *sent* your Self this moment as a gift. The moment contained the seed of a tremendous truth. It is a truth you wished to remember. Yet when the moment arrived, you immediately began constructing thoughts about it. Instead of being *in* the moment, you stood *outside* the moment and judged it. Then you re-acted. That is, you acted as you *did once before*.

Now look at these two words:

REACTIVE

CREATIVE

Notice they are the *same word*. Only the "C" has been moved! When you "C" things correctly, you become Creative, rather than Reactive.

That's very clever.

Well, God is like that.

But, you see, the point I am trying to make is that when you come to each moment cleanly, *without a previous thought about it*, you can *create* who you *are*, rather than *re-enact* who you *once were*.

Life is a process of creation, and you keep living it as if it were a process of re-enactment!

But how can any rational human being ignore one's previous experience in the moment something occurs? Isn't it normal to call up everything you know on the subject and respond from that?

It may be normal, but it is not *natural*. "Normal" means something usually done. "Natural" is how you are when you're not trying to be "normal"!

Natural and normal are not the same thing. In any given moment you can do what you normally do, or you can do what comes naturally.

I tell you this: *Nothing is more natural than love.*

If you act lovingly, you will be acting naturally. If you react fearfully, resentfully, angrily, you may be acting *normally*, but you will never be acting *naturally*.

How can I act with love when all my previous experience is screaming at me that a particular "moment" is likely to be painful?

Ignore your previous experience and *go into the moment*. Be Here Now. See what there is to work with *right now* in *creating yourself anew*.

Remember, *this is what you are doing here*.

You have come to this world in this way, at this time, in this place, to Know Who You Are—and to create Who You Wish to Be.

This is the purpose of all of life. Life is an ongoing, never-ending process of re-creation. You keep recreating your selves in the image of your next highest idea about yourselves.

But isn't that rather like the man who jumped off the highest building, sure that he could fly? He ignored his "previous experience" *and* the "observed experience of others" and jumped off the building, all the while declaring, "I am God!" That doesn't seem very smart.

And I tell you this: Men have achieved results much greater than flying. Men have healed sickness. Men have raised the dead.

One man has.

You think only one man has been granted such powers over the physical universe?

Only one man has demonstrated them.

Not so. Who parted the Red Sea?

God.

Indeed, but who called upon God to do that?

Moses.

Exactly. And who called upon Me to heal the sick, and raise the dead?

Jesus.

Yes. Now, do you think that what Moses and Jesus did, you *cannot* do?

But they didn't *do* it! They asked *You* to! That's a different thing.

Okay. We'll go with your construction for now. And do you think that *you* cannot ask Me these same miraculous things?

I suppose I could.

And would I grant them?

I don't know.

That's the difference between you and Moses! That's what separates you from Jesus!

Many people believe if they ask in Jesus' name, You *will* grant their request.

Yes, many people do believe that. They believe they have no power, but they have *seen* (or believe others who had seen) the power of Jesus, so they ask in his name. Even though he said, "Why are you so amazed? These things, and more, shall you also do." Yet the people could not believe it. Many do not to this day.

You all imagine you are unworthy. So you ask in the name of Jesus. Or the Blessed Virgin Mary. Or the "patron saint" of this or that. Or the Sun God. Or the spirit of the East. You'll use anybody's name—*anybody's*—but your own!

Yet I tell you this—*Ask and you shall receive. Seek and you shall find. Knock and it shall be opened unto you.*

Jump off the building and you shall fly.

There have been people who have levitated. Do you believe this?

Well, I've heard of it.

And people who have walked through walls. And even left their bodies.

Yes, yes. But I've never *seen* anybody walk through walls— and I don't suggest anyone try it. Nor do I think we should jump off buildings. That's probably not good for your health.

That man fell to his death not because he could not have flown if he were coming from the right state of Being but because he could *never* have demonstrated Godliness by trying to show himself as separate from you.

Please explain.

The man on the building lived in a world of self-delusion in which he imagined himself to be *other than the rest of you*. By declaring "I am God," he *began* his demonstration with a lie. He hoped to make himself separate. Larger. More powerful.

It was an act of the ego.

Ego—that which is separate, individual—can never duplicate or demonstrate that which is One.

By seeking to demonstrate that he was God, the man on the building demonstrated only his separateness, not his unity, with all things. Thus, he sought to demonstrate Godliness by demonstrating Ungodliness, and failed.

Jesus, on the other hand, demonstrated Godliness by demonstrating Unity—and seeing Unity and Wholeness wherever (and upon whomever) he looked. In this his consciousness and My consciousness were One, and, in such a state, whatever he called forth was made manifest in his Divine Reality in that Holy Moment.

I see. So all it takes is "Christ Consciousness" to perform miracles! Well, that should make things simple. . . .

Actually, it does. More simple than you think. And many have achieved such consciousness. Many have been Christed, not just Jesus of Nazareth.

You can be Christed, too.

How—?

By seeking to be. By choosing to be. But it is a choice you must make every day, every minute. It must become the very *purpose of your life.*

It *is* the purpose of your life—you simply do not know it. And even if you know it, even if you remember the exquisite reason for your very existence, you do not seem to know how to *get* there from where you are.

Yes, that is the case. So how *can* I get from where I am to where I want to be?

I tell you this—again: *Seek and ye shall find. Knock and it shall be opened unto you.*

I've been "seeking" and "knocking" for 35 years. You'll pardon me if I'm a little bored with that line.

If not to say, disillusioned, yes? But really, while I have to give you good grades for trying—an "A for effort," so to speak—I can't say, I can't agree with you, that you've been seeking and knocking for 35 years.

Let's agree that you've been seeking and knocking *on and off* for 35 years—mostly off.

In the past, when you were very young, you came to Me only when you were in trouble, when you needed something. As you grew older and matured, you realized that was probably not a *right relationship* with God, and sought to create something more meaningful. Even then, I was hardly more than a *sometimes thing.*

Still later, as you came to understand that *union* with God can be achieved only through *communion* with God, you undertook the practices and behaviors that could *achieve* communion, yet even these you engaged sporadically, inconsistently.

You meditated, you held ritual, you called Me forth in prayer and chant, you evoked the Spirit of Me in you, but only when it suited you, only when you felt inspired to.

And, glorious as your experience of Me was even on these occasions, still you've spent 95 percent of your life caught up in the illusion of *separateness*, and only flickering moments here and there in the realization of *ultimate reality*.

You still think your life is about car repairs and telephone bills and what you want out of relationships, that it's about the *dramas* you've created, rather than the *creator* of those dramas.

You have yet to learn *why* you keep creating your dramas. You're too busy playing them out.

You say you understand the meaning of life, but you do not live your understandings. You say you know the way toward communion with God, but you do not take that way. You claim you are on the *path*, but you do not walk it.

Then you come to Me and say you've been seeking and knocking for 35 years.

I hate to be the one to disillusion you, but. . . .

It's time you stopped being disillusioned in Me and started seeing *you* as you really are.

Now—I tell you this: You want to be "Christed"? *Act like Christ, every minute of every day.* (It's not that you don't know how. He has shown you the way.) Be like Christ in every circumstance. (It's not that you can't. He has left you *instructions*.)

You are not without help in this, should you seek it. I am giving you guidance every minute of every day. I Am the still small voice within which knows which way to turn, which path to take, which answer to give, which action to implement, which word to say—which *reality to create* if you truly seek communion and unity with Me.

Just *listen* to Me.

I guess I don't know how to do that.

Oh, nonsense! *You're doing it right now!* Simply do it *all the time.*

I can't walk around with a yellow legal pad every minute of the day. I can't stop everything and start writing notes to You, hoping You'll be there with one of Your brilliant answers.

> Thank you. They *are* brilliant! And here's another one: *Yes, you can!*
>
> I mean, if someone told you that you could have a direct Connection with God—a direct link, a direct line—and all you had to do was make sure you had paper and pen handy at all times, would you do it?

Well, yes, of *course.*

> Yet you just said you *wouldn't.* Or "can't." So what's the matter with you? What are you saying? What *is* your truth?
>
> Now the Good News is that you don't even *need* a pad and pen. *I am with you always.* I don't live in the pen. *I live in you.*

That *is* true, isn't it. . . . I mean, I can really believe that, can't I?

> Of course you can believe it. It's what I've been *asking* you to believe from the beginning. It's what every Master, including Jesus, has said to you. It is the central teaching. It is the ultimate truth.
>
> *I am with you always, even unto the end of time.*
>
> Do you believe this?

Yes, now I do. More than ever, I mean.

> Good. Then *use* Me. If it works for you to take out a pad and a pen (and, I must say, that seems to work pretty well for you), then *take out a pad and a pen.* More *often.* Every day. Every hour, if you have to.
>
> Get close to Me. *Get close to Me!* Do what you can. Do what you have to. Do what it takes.

Say a rosary. Kiss a stone. Bow to the East. Chant a chant. Swing a pendulum. Test a muscle.

Or write a book.

Do what it takes.

Each of you has your own construction. Each of you has understood Me—created Me—in your own way.

To some of you I am a man. To some of you I am a woman. To some, I am both. To some, I am neither.

To some of you I am pure energy. To some, the ultimate feeling, which you call love. And some of you have no idea what I am. You simply know that I AM.

And so it is.

I AM.

I am the wind which rustles your hair. I am the sun which warms your body. I am the rain which dances on your face. I am the smell of flowers in the air, and I am the flowers which send their fragrance upward. I am the air which *carries* the fragrance.

I am the beginning of your first thought. I am the end of your last. I am the idea which sparked your most brilliant moment. I am the glory of its fulfillment. I am the feeling which fueled the most loving thing you ever did. I am the part of you which yearns for that feeling again and again.

Whatever works for you, whatever makes it happen—*whatever* ritual, ceremony, demonstration, meditation, thought, song, word, or action it *takes* for you to "reconnect"—*do this.*

Do this in remembrance of Me.

3

So, going back and summarizing what you are telling me, I seem to come up with these main points.

- Life is an ongoing process of creation.

- A secret of all Masters is to stop changing one's mind; keep choosing the same thing.

- Don't take *no* for an answer.

- We "call forth" what we think, feel, and say.

- Life can be a process of creation or reaction.

- The soul *creates*, the mind *reacts*.

- The soul understands what the mind cannot conceive.

- Stop trying to figure out what is "best" for you (how you can win the most, lose the least, get what you want) and start going with what feels like Who You Are.

- Your feelings are your truth. What is best for you is what is true for you.

- Thoughts are *not* feelings; rather, they are ideas of how you "should" feel. When thoughts and feelings get confused, truth becomes clouded, lost.

- To get back to your feelings, be *out of your mind* and *get back to your senses.*

- Once you know your truth, *live* it.

- Negative feelings are not true feelings at all; rather, they are your thoughts about something, based always on the previous experience of yourself and others.

• Previous experience is no indicator of truth, since Pure Truth is created here and now, not reenacted.

• To change your response to anything, be in the present (that is, the "pre-sent") moment—the moment that was sent to you and was what it was before you had a thought about it. . . . In other words, Be Here Now, not in the past or the future.

• The past and the future can exist only in thought. The Pre-sent Moment is the Only Reality. *Stay* there!

• Seek and you shall find.

• Do whatever it takes to stay connected with God/Goddess/Truth. Don't stop the practices, the prayers, the rituals, the meditations, the readings, the writings, the *"whatever works" for you* to stay in touch with All That Is.

How's that so far?

> Great! So far, so good. You've got it. Now, can you live it?

I'm going to try.

> Good.

Yes. Now, can we go to where we left off? Tell me about Time.

> There *is* no Time like the pre-sent!
> You've heard that before, I'm sure. But you didn't understand it. Now you do.
> There is no time but *this* time. There is no moment but this moment. "Now" is all there is.

What about "yesterday" and "tomorrow"?

Figments of your imagination. Constructions of your mind. Nonexistent in Ultimate Reality.

Everything that ever happened, is happening, and ever will happen, is happening right *now*.

I don't understand.

And you can't. Not completely. But you can *begin* to. And a beginning grasp is all that is needed here.

So . . . just listen.

"Time" is not a continuum. It is an element of relativity that exists vertically, not horizontally.

Don't think of it as a "left to right" thing—a so-called time line that runs from birth to death for each individual, and *from* some finite point *to* some finite point for the universe.

"Time" is an "up and down" thing! Think of it as a spindle, representing the Eternal Moment of Now.

Now picture leafs of paper on the spindle, one atop the other. These are the elements of time. Each element separate and distinct, yet each existing *simultaneously with the other.* All the paper on the spindle at once! As much as there will ever *be*—as much as there ever *was.* . . .

There is only One Moment—*this* moment—the Eternal Moment of Now.

It is *right now* that everything is happening—and I am glorified. There is no waiting for the glory of God. I made it this way because *I just couldn't wait!* I was so *happy* to Be Who I Am that I just couldn't wait to make that manifest in My reality. So BOOM, here it is—right here, right now—ALL OF IT!

There is no Beginning to this, and there is no End. It—the All of Everything—just IS.

Within the Isness is where your experience—and your greatest secret—lies. You can move in consciousness within the Isness to any "time" or "place" you choose.

You mean we can time travel?

Indeed—and many of you have. *All* of you have, in fact—and you do it routinely, usually in what you call your dream state. Most of you are not aware of it. You cannot retain the awareness. But the energy sticks to you like glue, and sometimes there's enough residue that others—sensitive to this energy—can pick up things about your "past" or your "future." They feel or "read" this residue, and you call them seers and psychics. Sometimes there is enough residue that even you, in your limited consciousness, are aware you've "been here before." Your whole being is suddenly jarred by the realization that you've "done this all before"!

Déjà vu!

Yes. Or that wonderful feeling when you meet someone that you've *known them all your life*—known them for all *eternity!*

That's a spectacular feeling. That's a marvelous feeling. And that's a *true* feeling. You *have* known that soul *forever!*

Forever is a right now thing!

So you have *often* looked up, or looked down, from your "piece of paper" on the spindle, and seen all the other pieces! And you've seen yourself there—because *a part of You is on every piece!*

How is that possible?

I tell you this: You have always been, are now, and always will be. There has *never* been a time when you were not—nor will there ever *be* such a time.

But wait! What about the concept of *old souls*! Aren't some souls "older" than others?

Nothing is "older" than *anything*. I created it ALL AT ONCE, and All Of It exists *right now*.

The experience of "older" and "younger" to which you refer has to do with the *levels of awareness* of a particular soul, or Aspect of Being. You are all Aspects of Being, simply parts of What Is. Each part has the consciousness of the Whole imbedded within it. Every element carries the imprint.

"Awareness" is the experience of that consciousness being awakened. The individual aspect of the ALL becomes aware of Itself. It becomes, quite literally, *self conscious*.

Then, gradually, it becomes conscious of all others, and then, of the fact that there *are* no others—that All is One.

Then, ultimately, of Me. Magnificent Me!

Boy, You really *like* You, don't You?

Don't you—?

Yes, yes! I think You're great!

I agree. And I think *you're* great! That's the only place where You and I disagree. *You don't think you're great!*

How can I see myself as great when I see all my foibles, all my mistakes—all my evil?

I tell you this: There *is* no evil!

I wish that could be true.

You are perfect, just as you are.

I wish that could be true, too.

It *is* true! A tree is no less perfect because it is a seedling. A tiny infant is no less perfect than a grown-up.

It is *perfection itself.* Because it cannot *do* a thing, does not *know* a thing, that does not make it somehow less perfect.

A child makes mistakes. She stands. She toddles. She falls. She stands again, a bit wobbly, hanging on to her mommy's leg. Does that make the child imperfect?

I tell you it is just the opposite! That child is *perfection itself*, wholly and completely adorable.

So, too, are *you.*

But the child hasn't done anything wrong! The child hasn't consciously disobeyed, hurt another, damaged herself.

The child doesn't *know* right from wrong.

Precisely.

Neither do you.

But I *do.* I know that it is wrong to kill people, and that it is right to love them. I know that it is wrong to hurt and right to heal, to make things better. I know that it is wrong to take what is not mine, to use another, to be dishonest.

I could show you instances where each of those "wrongs" would be *right.*

You're playing with me now.

Not at all. Merely being factual.

If you are saying there are exceptions to every rule, then I agree.

If there are *exceptions* to a rule, then it is not a *rule.*

Are you telling me that it is *not* wrong to kill, to hurt, to take from another?

That depends on what you are trying to *do.*

Okay, okay, I get it. But that doesn't make these things *good*. Sometimes one has to do bad things to achieve a good end.

Which doesn't make them "bad things" at all, then, does it? They are just means to an end.

Are you saying the end justifies the means?

What do you think?

No. Absolutely not.

So be it.

Don't you see what you're doing here? You're *making up the rules as you go along!*

And don't you see something else? *That's perfectly okay.*

It's what you're *supposed* to be doing!

All of life is a process of deciding Who You Are, and then experiencing that.

As you keep expanding your vision, you make up new rules to cover that! As you keep enlarging your idea about your Self, you create new dos and don'ts, yeses and nos to encircle that. These are the boundaries that "hold in" something which *cannot* be held in.

You cannot hold in "you," because you are as boundless as the Universe. Yet you can create a *concept* about your boundless self by imagining, and then accepting, *boundaries.*

In a sense, this is the only way you can *know* yourself as anything in particular.

That which is boundless is boundless. That which is limitless is limitless. It cannot exist anywhere, because it is everywhere. If it is *everywhere*, it is *nowhere in particular.*

God is everywhere. Therefore, God is nowhere in particular, because to be somewhere in particular, God would have to *not be somewhere else*—which is *not possible for God.*

There is only one thing that is "not possible" for God, and that is for God to *not be God*. God cannot "not be." Nor can God not be like Itself. God cannot "un-God" Itself.

I am everywhere, and that's all there is to it. And since I am everywhere, I am nowhere. And if I am NOWHERE, where am I?

NOW HERE.

I love it! You made this point in the first book, but I love it, so I let You go on.

That's very kind of you. And do you understand it better now? Do you see how you have created your ideas of "right" and "wrong" simply to *define Who You Are?*

Do you see that without these definitions—boundaries—you are nothing?

And do you see that, like Me, you keep changing the boundaries as you change your Ideas of Who You Are?

Well, I get what You are saying, but it does not seem that I have changed the boundaries—my own personal boundaries—very much. To me it has always been wrong to kill. It has always been wrong to steal. It has always been wrong to hurt another. The largest concepts by which we govern ourselves have been in place since the beginning of time, and most human beings agree on them.

Then why do you have war?

Because there will always be some who break the rules. There's a rotten apple in every barrel.

What I'm going to tell you now, and in the passages which follow, may be very difficult for some people to understand and accept. It is going to violate much of what is held as truth in your present thought system. Yet I cannot let you go on living with these constructions if this dialogue is to serve you. So we must, now, in this second book, meet some of these concepts head on. But it's going to be bumpy going here for a while. Are you ready?

I think so, yes. Thanks for the warning. What is it that's so dramatic or difficult to understand or accept that You're going to tell me?

I am going to tell you this: there are *no* "rotten apples." There are only people who *disagree with your point of view on things,* people who construct a different model of the world. I am going to tell you this: No persons do anything inappropriate, given their model of the world.

Then their "model" is all messed up. *I* know what's right and wrong, and because some other people don't, that doesn't make *me* crazy because I *do. They're* the ones who are crazy!

I'm sorry to say that's exactly the attitude which starts wars.

I know, I know. I was doing that on purpose. I was just repeating here what I've heard many other people say. But how *can* I answer people like that? What *could* I say?

You could tell them that people's ideas of "right" and "wrong" change—and have changed—over and over again from culture to culture, time period to time period, religion to religion, place to place . . . even from family to family and person to person. You could point out to them that what many people considered "right" at one time— burning people at the stake for what was considered witchcraft, as an example—is considered "wrong" today.

You could tell them that a definition of "right" and "wrong" is a definition established not only by time, but also by simple geography. You could allow them to notice that some activities on your planet (prostitution, for instance) are illegal in one place, and, just a few miles down the road, legal in another. And so, whether a person is judged as having done something "wrong" is not a matter of what that person has actually *done*, but of *where he has done it.*

Now I am going to repeat something I said in *Book 1*, and I know that it was very, very difficult for some to grasp, to understand.

Hitler went to heaven.

I'm not sure people are ready for this.

The purpose of this book, and of all the books in the trilogy we are creating, is to create readiness—readiness for a new paradigm, a new understanding; a larger view, a grander idea.

Well, I'm going to have to ask the questions here that I know so many people are thinking and wanting to ask. How could a man like Hitler have gone to heaven? Every religion in the world . . . I would think *every* one, has declared him condemned and sent straight to hell.

First, he could not have gone to hell because hell does not exist. Therefore, there is only one place left to which he *could* have gone. But that begs the question. The real issue is whether Hitler's actions where "wrong." Yet I have said over and over again that there is no "right" or "wrong" in the universe. A thing is not intrinsically right or wrong. A thing simply *is.*

Now your thought that Hitler was a monster is based on the fact that he ordered the killing of millions of people, correct?

Obviously, yes.

Yet what if I told you that what you call "death" is *the greatest thing that could happen to anyone*—what then?

I'd find that hard to accept.

> You think that life on Earth is better than life in heaven? I tell you this, at the moment of your death you will realize the greatest freedom, the greatest peace, the greatest joy, and the greatest love you have ever known. Shall we therefore punish Bre'r Fox for throwing Bre'r Rabbit into the briar patch?

You are ignoring the fact that, however wonderful life after death may be, our lives here should not be ended against our will. We came here to achieve something, to experience something, to learn something, and it is not right that our lives be cut short by some maniacal hoodlum with insane ideas.

> First of all, you are not here to *learn anything*. (Reread *Book 1*!) Life is not a school, and your purpose here is not to learn; it is to remember. And on your larger point, life is often "cut short" by many things . . . a hurricane, an earthquake. . . .

That's different. You're talking about an Act of God.

> *Every* event is an Act of God.
> Do you imagine that an event could take place if I did not want it to? Do you think that you could so much as lift your little finger if I chose for you not to? You can do *nothing* if I am against it.
> Yet let us continue to explore this idea of "wrongful" death together. Is it "wrong" for a life to be cut short by disease?

"Wrong" isn't a word that applies here. Those are natural causes. That's not the same as a human being like Hitler murdering people.

> What about an accident? A stupid accident—?

Same thing. It's unfortunate, tragic, but that's the Will of God. We can't peer into God's mind and find out why these things happen. We ought not try, because God's Will is immutable and incomprehensible. To seek to unravel Divine Mystery is to lust for knowledge beyond our ken. It is sinful.

How do you know?

Because if God wanted us to understand all of this, we *would*. The fact that we *don't—can't*—is evidence that it is God's *will* that we don't.

I see. The fact that you don't *understand* it is evidence of God's Will. The fact that it *happens* is *not* evidence of God's Will. Hmmmm. . . .

I guess I'm not very good at explaining some of this, but I know what I believe.

Do you believe in God's Will, that God is All Powerful?

Yes.

Except where Hitler was concerned. What happened there was *not* God's Will.

No.

How can that be?

Hitler violated the Will of God.

Now how do you think he could do that if My Will is all powerful?

You allowed him to.

If I *allowed* him to, then it was My *Will* that he should.

It would seem that way . . . but what possible *reason* could You have? No. It was Your Will that he have Free Choice. It was *his* will that he do what he did.

> You're so close on this. So close.
>
> You're right, of course. It was My Will that Hitler—that *all* of you—have Free Choice. But it is *not* My Will that you be punished unceasingly, unendingly, if you do not make the choice I want you to make. If that were the case, how "free" have I made *your* choice? Are you really free to do what you want if you know you'll be made to suffer unspeakably if you do not do what *I* want? What kind of choice is that?

It isn't a question of punishment. It's just Natural Law. It's simply a question of consequences.

> I see you've been schooled well in all the theological constructions that allow you to hold Me as a vengeful God—without making Me responsible for it.
>
> But who *made* these Natural Laws? And if we can agree that *I* must have put them into place, why would I put into place such laws—then give you the power to overcome them?
>
> If I didn't want you affected by them—if it was My Will that My wonderful beings never should suffer—why would I create the *possibility* that you could?
>
> And then, why would I continue to tempt you, day and night, to break the laws I've set down?

You don't tempt us. The devil does.

> There you go again, making Me not responsible.
>
> Don't you see that the only way you can rationalize your theology is to render Me powerless? Do you understand that the only way your constructions make sense is if Mine *don't?*

Are you really comfortable with the idea of a God who creates a being whose actions it cannot control?

I didn't say You can't control the devil. You can control *every-thing*. You're *God!* It's just that You *choose not to.* You *allow* the devil to tempt us, to try to win our souls.

But *why?* Why would I *do* that if I don't *want* to have you not return to Me?

Because You want us to come to You out of choice, not because there is no choice. You set up Heaven and Hell so there could be a choice. So we could act out of choosing, and not out of simply following a path because there is no other.

I can see how you've come to this idea. That's how I've set it up in your world, and so you think that's how it must be in *Mine*.

In your reality, Good cannot exist without Bad. So you believe it must be the same in Mine.

Yet I tell you this: There *is* no "bad" where I Am. And there is no Evil. There is only the All of Everything. The Oneness. And the Awareness, the Experience, of that.

Mine is the Realm of the Absolute, where One Thing does not exist in relationship to Another, but quite independent of anything.

Mine is the place where All There Is is Love.

And there are no consequences to anything we think, say or do on Earth?

Oh, but there *are* consequences. Look around you.

I mean after death.

There is no "death." Life goes on forever and ever. Life Is. You simply change form.

All right, have it Your way—after we "change form."

After you change form, consequences cease to exist. There is just Knowing.

Consequences are an element of relativity. They have no place in the Absolute because they depend on linear "time" and sequential events. These do not exist in the Realm of the Absolute.

In that realm there is naught but peace and joy and love.

In that realm you will know at last the Good News: that your "devil" does not exist, that you are who you always thought you were—goodness and love. Your idea that you might be something else has come from an insane outer world, causing you to act insanely. An outer world of judgment and condemnation. Others have judged you, and from their judgments you have judged yourself.

Now you want God to judge you, and I will not do it.

And because you cannot understand a God who will not act as humans would, you are lost.

Your theology is your attempt to find yourself again.

You call our theologies insane—but how can any theology work without a system of Reward and Punishment?

Everything depends on what you perceive to be the purpose of life—and therefore the basis of the theology.

If you believe life exists as a test, a trial, a period of putting you through your paces to see if you are "worthy," your theologies begin to make sense.

If you believe that life exists as an *opportunity*, a process through which you discover—remember—that you *are* worthy (and have *always* been), then your theologies seem insane.

If you believe God is an ego-filled God who requires attention, adoration, appreciation, and affection—*and will kill to get it*—your theologies start to hold together.

If you believe that God is without ego or need, but the *source* of all things, and the seat of all wisdom and love, then your theologies fall apart.

If you believe that God is a vengeful God, jealous in His love and wrathful in His anger, then your theologies are perfect.

If you believe God is a peaceful God, joyous in Her love and passionate in Her ecstasy, then your theologies are useless.

I tell you this: the purpose of life is not to please God. The purpose of life is to know, and to recreate, Who You Are.

In so doing you *do* please God, and glorify *Her* as well.

Why do you keep saying "Her"? Are you a She?

I am neither a "he" *nor* a "she." I occasionally use the feminine pronoun to jar you out of your parochial thinking.

If you think God is one thing, then you will think God is not another. And that would be a large mistake.

Hitler went to heaven for these reasons:

There is no hell, so there is no place else for him to go.

His actions were what you would call mistakes—the actions of an unevolved being—and mistakes are not punishable by condemnation, but dealt with by providing the chance for correction, for evolution.

The mistakes Hitler made did no harm or damage to those whose deaths he caused. Those souls were released from their earthly bondage, like butterflies emerging from a cocoon.

The people who were left behind mourn those deaths only because they do not know of the joy into which those souls entered. No one who has experienced death *ever mourns the death of anyone.*

Your statement that their deaths were nevertheless untimely, and therefore somehow "wrong," suggests that something could happen in the universe *when it is not supposed to.* Yet given Who and What I Am, that is impossible.

Everything occurring in the universe is occurring perfectly. God hasn't made a mistake in a very long time.

When you see the utter perfection in everything—not just those things with which you agree, but (and perhaps especially) those things with which you disagree—you achieve mastery.

I know all of this, of course. We've been through all of this in *Book 1.* But for those who have not read *Book 1,* I thought it important to have a basis of understanding early in this book. That's why I've led into this series of questions and answers. But now, before we go on, I'd like to talk just a bit more about some of the very complex theologies we human beings have created. For instance, I was taught as a child that I was a sinner, that all human beings are sinners, that we can't help it; we're born that way. We're born *into sin.*

Quite an interesting concept. How did anyone get you to believe that?

They told us the story of Adam and Eve. They told us in 4th, 5th, and 6th grade catechism that, well, *we* may not have sinned, and certainly *babies* haven't—but Adam and Eve *did*—and we are their descendants and have thus inherited their guilt, as well as their sinful natures.

You see, Adam and Eve ate of the forbidden fruit—partook of the knowledge of Good and Evil—and thus sentenced all of their heirs and descendants to separation from God at birth. All of us are born with this "Original Sin" on our souls. Each of us shares in the guilt. So we are given Free Choice to see, I guess, if we will do the same stuff as Adam and Eve and disobey God, or if we can overcome our natural, inherited tendency to "do bad," and do the right things instead, in spite of the world's temptations.

And if you do "bad"?

Then You send us to hell.

I do?

Yes. Unless we repent.

I see.

If we say we're sorry—make a Perfect Act of Contrition— You'll save us from Hell—but not from *all* suffering. We'll still have to go to Purgatory for a while, to cleanse us of our sins.

How long will you have to dwell in "Purgatory"?

Depends. We have to have our sins burned away. It's not too pleasant, I can tell you. And the more sins we've got, the longer it takes to burn them out—the longer we stay. That's what I've been told.

I understand.

But at least we won't go to hell, which is forever. On the other hand, if we die in mortal sin, we go *straight* to hell.

Mortal sin?

As opposed to venial sin. If we die with a venial sin on our soul, we only go to Purgatory. Mortal sin sends us right to hell.

Can you give me an example of these various categories of sin you were told about?

Sure. Mortal sins are serious. Kind of like Major Crimes. Theological Felonies. Things like murder, rape, stealing. Venial sins are rather minor. Theological Misdemeanors. A venial sin would be like missing church on Sunday. Or, in the old days, eating meat on Friday.

Wait a minute! This God of yours sent you to Purgatory if you ate meat on Friday?

Yes. But not any more. Not since the early sixties. But if we ate meat on Fridays *before* the early sixties, woe be unto us.

Really?

Absolutely.

Well, what happened in the early sixties to make this "sin" no longer a sin?

The Pope said it was no longer a sin.

I see. And this God of yours—He *forces* you to worship Him, to go to church on Sundays? Under pain of punishment?

Failure to attend Mass is a sin, yes. And if not confessed—if you die with that sin on your soul—you'll have to go to Purgatory.

But—what about a child? What about an innocent little child who doesn't know all these "rules" by which God loves?

Well, if a child dies before it is baptized into the faith, that child goes to Limbo.

Goes to *where?*

Limbo. It's not a place of punishment, but it's not heaven, either. It's . . . well . . . *limbo.* You can't be with God, but at least you don't have to "go to the devil."

But why couldn't that beautiful, innocent child be with God? The child did nothing *wrong.* . . .

That's true, but the child was not baptized. No matter how faultless or innocent babies are—or any persons, for that matter—they have to be baptized to get into heaven. Otherwise God can't accept them. That's why it's important to have your children baptized quickly, soon after birth.

Who told you all this?

God. Through His church.

Which church?

The Holy Roman Catholic Church, of course. That *is* God's church. In fact, if you are a Catholic and you should happen to attend *another* church, that's also a sin.

I thought it was a sin *not* to go to church!

It is. It's also a sin to go to the *wrong* church.

What's a "wrong" church?

Any church that is not Roman Catholic. You can't be baptized in the wrong church, you can't get married in the wrong church—you can't even *attend* a wrong church. I know this for a fact because as a young man I wanted to go with my parents to the wedding of a friend—I was actually asked to be *in* the wedding as an usher—but the nuns told me I should not accept the invitation because it was in the *wrong church.*

Did you obey them?

The nuns? No. I figured God—You—would show up at the other church just as willingly as You showed up at mine, so I went. I stood in the sanctuary in my tuxedo and I felt fine.

Good. Well, let's see now, we have heaven, we have hell, we have purgatory, we have limbo, we have mortal sin, we have venial sin—is there anything else?

Well, there's confirmation and communion and confession—there's exorcism and Extreme Unction. There's—

Hold it—

—there's Patron Saints and Holy Days of Obligation—

Every day is sanctified. Every *minute* is holy. *This, now,* is the *Holy Instant.*

Well, yes, but some days are *really* holy—the Holy Days of Obligation—and on those days we also have to go to church.

Here we go with the "have tos" again. And what happens if you don't?

It's a sin.

So you go to hell.

Well, you go to Purgatory if you die with that sin on your soul. That's why it's good to go to Confession. Really, as often as you can. Some people go every week. Some people every *day.* That way they can wipe the slate clean—keep it clean so if they should happen to die. . . .

Wow—talk about living in constant fear.

Yes, you see, that's the purpose of religion—to put the fear of God into us. Then we do right and resist temptation.

Uh-huh. But now, what if you do commit a "sin" between confessions, and then get into an accident or something, and die?

It's okay. No panic. Just make a Perfect Act of Contrition. "Oh, my God, I am heartily sorry for having offended Thee . . ."

Okay, okay—enough.

But wait. That's just one of the world's religions. Don't You want to look at some others?

No, I get the picture.

Well, I hope that people don't think I'm simply ridiculing their beliefs.

You're really ridiculing no one, just saying it like it is. It's as your American President Harry Truman used to say. "Give 'em hell, Harry!" people would shout, and Harry'd say, "I don't give 'em hell. I just quote 'em directly, and it *feels* like hell."

4

Boy, we really got sidetracked there. We started out talking about Time and ended up talking about organized religion.

Yes, well, that's what it's like talking with God. It's hard to keep the dialogue limited.

Let me see if I can summarize the points You make in chapter 3.

- There is no time but *this* time; there is no moment but *this* moment.

- Time is not a continuum. It is an aspect of Relativity that exists in an "up and down" paradigm, with "moments" or "events" stacked on top of each other, happening or occurring at the same "time."

- We are constantly traveling between realities in this realm of time–no time–all time, usually in our sleep. *"Déjà vu"* is one way we are made aware of this.

- There has never been a time when we were "not"— nor will there ever be.

- The concept of "Age" as it relates to souls really has to do with levels of awareness, not length of "time."

- There is no evil.

- We are Perfect, just as we are.

- "Wrong" is a conceptualization of the mind, based in Relative Experience.

- We are making up the rules as we go along, changing them to fit our Present Reality, and that's perfectly all right. It's as it should be, *must* be, if we are to be evolving beings.

- Hitler went to heaven(!)

- Everything that happens is God's Will—*everything*. That includes not just hurricanes, tornadoes, and earthquakes, but Hitler as well. The secret of understanding is knowing the *Purpose* behind all events.

- There are no "punishments" after death, and all consequences exist only in Relative Experience, not in the Realm of the Absolute.

- Human theologies are mankind's insane attempt to explain an insane God who does not exist.

- The only way human theologies make sense is if we accept a God who makes no sense at all.

How's that? Another good summary?

Excellent.

Good. Because now I've got a million questions. Statements 10 and 11, for instance, beg for further clarification. Why *did* Hitler go to heaven? (I know You just tried to explain this, but somehow I need more.) And what *is* the purpose behind all events? And how does this Larger Purpose relate to Hitler and other despots?

Let's go to Purpose first.

All events, all experiences, have as their purpose the creating of *opportunity*. Events and experiences are Opportunities. Nothing more, nothing less.

It would be a mistake to judge them as "works of the devil," "punishments from God," "rewards from Heaven," or anything in between. They are simply Events and Experiences—things that happen.

It is what we *think* of them, *do* about them, *be* in response to them, that gives them meaning.

62

Events and experiences are opportunities drawn to you—created *by* you individually or collectively, through consciousness. Consciousness creates experience. You are attempting to raise your consciousness. You have drawn these opportunities to you in order that you might use them as tools in the creation and experiencing of Who You Are. Who You Are is a being of higher consciousness than you are now exhibiting.

Because it is My Will that you should know, and experience, Who You Are, I allow you to draw to yourself whatever event or experience you choose to create in order to do that.

Other Players in the Universal Game join you from time to time—either as Brief Encounters, Peripheral Participants, Temporary Teammates, Long-Term Interactors, Relatives and Family, Dearly Loved Ones, or Life Path Partners.

These souls are drawn to you *by* you. You are drawn to them *by* them. It is a mutually creative experience, expressing the choices and desires of both.

No one comes to you by accident.

There is no such thing as coincidence.

Nothing occurs at random.

Life is not a product of chance.

Events, like people, are drawn to you, by you, for your own purposes. Larger planetary experiences and developments are the result of group consciousness. They are drawn to your group as a whole as a result of the choices and desires of the group as a whole.

What do You mean by the term "your group"?

Group consciousness is something that is not widely understood—yet it is extremely powerful and can, if you are not careful, often overcome individual consciousness. You must always, therefore, endeavor to create group consciousness wherever you go, and with whatever you do, if you wish your larger life experience on the planet to be harmonious.

If you are in a group whose consciousness does not reflect your own, and you are unable at this time to effectively alter the group consciousness, it is wise to leave the group, or the group could lead *you*. It will go where *it* wants to go, regardless of where you want to go.

If you cannot find a group whose consciousness matches your own, be the *source* of one. Others of like consciousness will be drawn to you.

Individuals and smaller groups must affect larger groups—and, ultimately, the largest group of all, which is ALL humankind—for there to be permanent and significant change on your planet.

Your world, and the condition it is in, is a reflection of the total, combined consciousness of everyone living there.

As you can see by looking around you, much work is left to be done. Unless of course, you are satisfied with your world as it is.

Surprisingly, *most people are*. That is why the world does not change.

Most people *are* satisfied with a world in which differences, not similarities, are honored, and disagreements are settled by conflict and war.

Most people are satisfied with a world in which survival is for the fittest, "might is right," competition is required, and winning is called the highest good.

If such a system happens also to produce "losers"—so be it—so long as you are not among them.

Most people *are* satisfied, even though such a model produces people who are often killed when they are judged "wrong," starved and rendered homeless when they are "losers," oppressed and exploited when they are not "strong."

Most people define "wrong" as that which is different from them. Religious differences, in particular, are not tolerated, nor are many social, economic, or cultural differences.

Exploitation of the underclass is justified by the self-congratulatory pronouncements from the upper class of how much better off their victims are now than they were before these exploitations. By this measure the upper class can ignore the issue of how all people *ought* to be treated if one were being truly *fair,* rather than merely making a horrible situation a tiny bit better—and profiting obscenely in the bargain.

Most people *laugh* when one suggests any kind of system other than the one currently in place, saying that behaviors such as competing and killing and the "victor taking the spoils" are what makes their civilization *great!* Most people even think there is no other natural way to *be,* that it is the *nature* of humans to behave in this manner, and that to act any other way would kill the inner spirit that drives man to succeed. (No one asks the question, "Succeed at *what?*")

Difficult as it is for truly enlightened beings to understand, most people on your planet believe in this philosophy, and that is why most people don't *care* about the suffering masses, the oppression of minorities, the anger of the underclass, or the *survival* needs of anyone but themselves and their immediate families.

Most people do not see that they are destroying their Earth—the very planet which gives them *Life*—because their actions seek only to enhance their quality of life. Amazingly, they are not far-sighted enough to observe that short-term gains can produce long-term losses, and often do—and will.

Most people are *threatened* by group consciousness, a concept such as the collective good, a one-world overview, or a God who exists in unity with all creation, rather than separate from it.

This fear of anything leading to unification and your planet's glorification of All That Separates produces division, disharmony, discord—yet you do not seem to have the ability even to learn from your own experience, and so you continue your behaviors, with the same results.

The inability to experience the suffering of another as one's own is what allows such suffering to continue.

Separation breeds indifference, false superiority. Unity produces compassion, genuine equality.

The events which occur on your planet—which have occurred regularly for 3,000 years—are, as I've said, a reflection of the Collective Consciousness of "your group"—the whole group on your planet.

That level of consciousness could best be described as primitive.

Hmmm. Yes. But we seem to have digressed here from the original question.

Not really. You asked about Hitler. The Hitler Experience was made possible as a result of group consciousness. Many people want to say that Hitler manipulated a group—in this case, his countrymen—through the cunning and the mastery of his rhetoric. But this conveniently lays all the blame at Hitler's feet—which is exactly where the mass of the people want it.

But Hitler could do nothing without the cooperation and support and willing submission of millions of people. The subgroup which called itself Germans must assume an enormous burden of responsibility for the Holocaust. As must, to some degree, the larger group called Humans, which, if it did nothing else, allowed itself to remain indifferent and apathetic to the suffering in Germany until it reached so massive a scale that even the most cold-hearted isolationists could no longer ignore it.

You see, it was *collective consciousness* which provided fertile soil for the growth of the Nazi movement. Hitler seized the moment, but he did not create it.

It's important to understand the *lesson* here. A group consciousness which speaks constantly of separation and superiority produces loss of compassion on a massive scale, and loss of compassion is inevitably followed by loss of conscience.

A collective concept rooted in strict nationalism ignores the plights of others, yet makes everyone else responsible for *yours*, thus justifying retaliation, "rectification," and war.

Auschwitz was the Nazi solution to—an attempt to "rectify"—the "Jewish Problem."

The horror of the Hitler Experience was not that he perpetrated it on the human race, but that *the human race allowed him to.*

The astonishment is not only that a Hitler came along, but also that so many others *went* along.

The shame is not only that Hitler killed millions of Jews, but also that millions of Jews *had* to be killed before Hitler was stopped.

The purpose of the Hitler Experience was to show humanity to itself.

Throughout history you have had remarkable teachers, each presenting extraordinary opportunities to remember Who You Really Are. These teachers have shown you the highest and the lowest of the human potential.

They have presented vivid, breathtaking examples of what it can mean to be human—of where one can go with the experience, of where the *lot* of you can and *will* go, *given your consciousness.*

The thing to remember: Consciousness is everything, and creates your experience. *Group* consciousness is powerful and produces outcomes of unspeakable beauty or ugliness. The choice is always yours.

If you are not satisfied with the consciousness of your group, seek to change it.

The best way to change the consciousness of others is by your example.

If your example is not enough, form your own group—*you* be the *source* of the consciousness you wish others to experience. They *will*—when you do.

It begins with *you*. Everything. All things.

You want the world to change? Change things in your own world.

Hitler gave you a golden opportunity to do that. The Hitler Experience—like the Christ Experience—is profound in its implications and the truths it revealed to you *about* you. Yet those larger awarenesses live—in the case of Hitler *or* Buddha, Genghis Kahn *or* Hare Krishna, Attila the Hun or Jesus the Christ—only so long as your memories of them live.

That is why Jews build monuments to the Holocaust and ask you never to forget it. For there is a little bit of Hitler in all of you—and it is only a matter of degree. Wiping out a people is wiping out a people, whether at Auschwitz or Wounded Knee.

So Hitler was sent to us to provide us a lesson about the horrors man can commit, the levels to which man can sink?

Hitler was not sent to you. Hitler was created *by* you. He arose out of your Collective Consciousness, and could not have existed without it. *That* is the lesson.

The consciousness of separation, segregation, superiority—of "we" versus "they," of "us" and "them"—is what creates the Hitler Experience.

The consciousness of Divine Brotherhood, of unity, of Oneness, of "ours" rather than "yours"/"mine," is what creates the Christ Experience.

When the pain is "ours," not just "yours," when the joy is "ours," not just "mine," when the *whole life experience* is Ours, then it is at last truly that—a Whole Life experience.

Why did Hitler go to heaven?

Because Hitler did nothing "wrong." Hitler simply did what he did. I remind you again that for many years millions thought he was "right." How, then, could he help but think so?

If you float out a crazy idea, and ten million people agree with you, you might not think you're so crazy.

The world decided—finally—that Hitler was "wrong." That is to say, the world's people made a new assessment of Who They Are, and Who They Chose To Be, in relationship to the Hitler Experience.

He held up a yardstick! He set a parameter, a border against which we could measure and limit our ideas about ourselves. Christ did the same thing, at the other end of the spectrum.

There have been other Christs, and other Hitlers. And there will be again. Be ever vigilant, then. For people of both high and low consciousness walk among you—even as *you* walk among others. Which consciousness do you take with you?

I still don't understand how Hitler could have gone to heaven; how he could have been *rewarded* for what he did?

First, understand that death is not an end, but a beginning; not a horror, but a joy. It is not a closing down, but an opening up.

The happiest moment of your life will be the moment it ends.

That's because it *doesn't* end but only goes on in ways so magnificent, so full of peace and wisdom and joy, as to make it difficult to describe and impossible for you to comprehend.

So the first thing you have to understand—as I've already explained to you—is that Hitler didn't *hurt* anyone. In a sense, he didn't *inflict* suffering, he *ended* it.

It was the Buddha who said "Life is suffering." The Buddha was right.

But even if I accept that—Hitler didn't *know* he was actually doing *good*. He thought he was doing *bad!*

No, he didn't think he was doing something "bad." He actually thought he was helping his people. And that's what you don't understand.

No one does *anything* that is "wrong," given their model of the world. If you think Hitler acted insanely and all the while *knew* that he was insane, then you understand nothing of the complexity of human experience.

Hitler thought he was doing *good* for his people. And his people thought so, too! *That was the insanity of it!* The largest part of the nation *agreed with him!*

You have declared that Hitler was "wrong." Good. By this measure you have come to define yourself, know more about yourself. Good. But don't condemn Hitler for *showing you that.*

Someone had to.

You cannot know cold unless there is hot, up unless there is down, left unless there is right. Do not condemn the one and bless the other. To do so is to fail to understand.

For centuries people have been condemning Adam and Eve. They are said to have committed Original Sin. I tell you this: It was the Original Blessing. For without this event, the partaking of the knowledge of good and evil, *you* would not even know the two possibilities existed! Indeed, before the so-called Fall of Adam, these two possibilities *did not* exist. There *was* no "evil." Everyone and everything existed in a state of constant perfection. It was, literally, paradise. Yet you didn't *know* it was paradise— could not *experience* it as perfection—because you *knew nothing else.*

Shall you then condemn Adam and Eve, or thank them?

And what, say you, shall I do with Hitler?

I tell you this: God's love and God's compassion, God's wisdom and God's forgiveness, God's intention and God's *purpose,* are large enough to include the most heinous crime and the most heinous criminal.

You may not agree with this, but it does not matter. You have just learned what you came here to discover.

5

You promised in the first book to explain in *Book 2* a long list of larger things—such as time and space, love and war, good and evil, and planetary geopolitical considerations of the highest order. You also promised to further explain—in some detail—the human experience of sex.

Yes, I promised all those things.

Book 1 had to do with more personal inquiries; with one's life as an individual. *Book 2* deals with your collective life on the planet. *Book 3* concludes the Trilogy with the largest truths: the cosmology, the whole picture, the journey of the soul. Taken together, My best current advice and information on everything from tying your shoe to understanding your universe.

Have You said all You're going to say about time?

I've said all you need to know.

There is no time. All things exist simultaneously. All events occur at once.

This Book is being written, and as it's being written it's *already* written; it already exists. In fact, that's where you're getting all this information—from the book that already exists. You're merely bringing it into form.

This is what is meant by: "Even before you ask, I will have answered."

This information about Time all seems . . . well, interesting, but rather esoteric. Does it have any application to real life?

A true understanding of time allows you to live much more peacefully within your reality of relativity, where time is experienced as a movement, a flow, rather than a constant.

It is *you* who are moving, not time. Time *has* no movement. There is only One Moment.

At some level you deeply understand this. That is why, when something really magnificent or significant occurs in your life, you often say it is as if "time stands still."

It *does*. And when *you do also*, you often experience one of those life-defining moments.

I find this hard to believe. How can this be possible?

Your science has already *proven* this mathematically. Formulas have been written showing that if you get into a spaceship and fly far enough *fast* enough, you could swing back around toward the Earth and *watch yourself taking off.*

This demonstrates that Time is not a *movement* but a field through which *you* move—in this case on Spaceship Earth.

You say it takes 365 "days" to make a year. Yet what is a "day"? You've decided—quite arbitrarily, I might add—that a "day" is the "time" it takes your Spaceship to make one complete revolution on its axis.

How do you know it's made such a spin? (You can't *feel* it moving!) You've chosen a reference point in the heavens—the Sun. You say it takes a full "day" for the portion of the Spaceship you are on to face the Sun, turn away from the Sun, then face the Sun again.

You've divided this "day" into 24 "hours"—again quite arbitrarily. You could just as easily have said "10" or "73"!

Then you divided each "hour" into "minutes." You said each hourly unit contained 60 smaller units, called "minutes"—and that each of *those* contained 60 tiny units, called "seconds."

One day you noticed that the Earth was not only spinning, it was also *flying!* You saw that it was moving through space *around the sun.*

You carefully calculated that it took 365 revolutions of the Earth for the Earth itself to revolve around the sun. This number of Earth spins you called a "year."

Things got kind of messy when you decided that you wanted to divide up a "year" into units smaller than a "year" but larger than a "day."

You created the "week" and the "month," and you managed to get the same number of months in every year, but not the same number of *days in every month.*

You couldn't find a way to divide an odd number of days (365) by an even number of months (12), so you just decided that *some months contained more days than others!*

You felt you had to stay with twelve as the yearly subdivider because that was the number of Lunar Cycles you observed your moon moving through during a "year." In order to reconcile these three spatial events—revolutions around the sun, spins of the Earth on its axis, and moon cycles—you simply adjusted the number of "days" in each "month."

Even this device didn't solve all the problems because your earlier inventions kept creating a "build up" of "time" which you didn't know what to do with. So you also decided that every so often one year would have to have a *whole day more!* You called this Leap Year, and joked about it, but you actually *live* by such a construction—and then you call *My* explanation of time "unbelievable"!

You've just as arbitrarily created "decades" and "centuries" (based, interestingly, on 10's, *not* 12's) to further measure the passage of "time"—but all along what you've really been doing is merely devising a way to measure *movements through space.*

Thus we see that it is not time which "passes," but *objects* which pass *through,* and move around *in,* a static field which you call *space.* "Time" is simply your way of *counting movements!*

Scientists deeply understand this connection and therefore speak in terms of the "Space-Time Continuum."

Your Dr. Einstein and others realized that time was a mental construction, a *relational concept.* "Time" was what it was *relative to the space* that existed between objects! (If the universe is expanding—which it is—then it takes "longer" for the Earth to revolve around the sun today than it did a billion years ago. There's more "space" to cover.)

Thus, it took more minutes, hours, days, weeks, months, years, decades, and centuries for all these cyclical events to occur recently than it did in 1492! (When is a "day" not a day? When is a "year" not a year?)

Your new, highly sophisticated timing instruments now record this "time" discrepancy, and every year clocks around the world are adjusted to accommodate a universe that won't sit still! This is called Greenwich Mean Time . . . and it is "mean" because it makes a liar out of the universe!

Einstein theorized that if it wasn't "time" which was moving, but *he* who was moving through space at a given rate, all he had to do was change the amount of space between objects—or change the rate of *speed* with which he moved through space from one object to another—to "alter" time.

It was his General Theory of Relativity which expanded your modern day understanding of the co-relation between time and space.

You now may begin to understand why, if you make a long journey through space and return, you may have aged only ten years—while your friends on Earth will have aged thirty! The farther you go, the more you will warp the Space-Time Continuum, and the less your chances when you land of finding alive on the Earth anyone who was there when you left!

However, if scientists on Earth in some "future" time developed a way to propel themselves *faster*, they could "cheat" the universe and stay in sync with "real time" on Earth, returning to find that the same time had passed on Earth as had passed on the Spaceship.

Obviously, if even more propulsion were available, one could return to the Earth before one took off! That is to say, time on Earth would pass *more slowly* than time on the spaceship. You could come back in ten of your "years" and the Earth would have "aged" only four! Increase the speed, and ten years in space might mean ten minutes on Earth.

Now, come across a "fold" in the fabric of space (Einstein and others believed such "folds" exist—and they were correct!) and you are suddenly propelled across "space" in one infinitesimal "moment." Could such a time-space phenomenon literally "fling" you back into "time"?

It should not be quite as difficult to now see that "time" does not exist except as a construction of your mentality. Everything that's ever happened—and is ever *going* to happen—is happening *now*. The ability to observe it merely depends on your point of view—your "place in space."

If you were in *My* place, you could see it All—*right now!*

Comprehend?

Wow! I'm *beginning* to—on a theoretical level—*yes!*

Good. I've explained it to you here very simply, so that a child could understand it. It may not make good science, but it produces good comprehension.

Right now physical objects are limited in terms of their speed—but *nonphysical objects*—my thoughts . . . my soul . . . could theoretically move through the ether at incredible speeds.

Exactly! *Precisely!* And that is what happens often in dreams and other out-of-body and psychic experiences.

You now understand *Déjà vu.* You probably *have* been there before!

But . . . if everything has already *happened*, then it follows that I am powerless to change my future. Is this predestination?

No! Don't buy into that! That is not true. In fact, this "set up" should *serve* you, not *disserve* you!

You are always at a place of free will and total choice. Being able to see into the "future" (or get others to do it for you) should enhance your ability to live the life you want, not limit it.

How? I need help here.

If you "see" a future event or experience you do not like, don't *choose* it! Choose again! Select another!

Change or alter your behavior so as to *avoid the undesired outcome.*

But how can I avoid that which has already happened?

It has not happened to you—yet! You are at a place in the Space-Time Continuum where you are not *consciously aware* of the occurrence. You do not "know" it has "happened." You have not "remembered" your future!

(This forgetfulness is the *secret of all time.* It is what makes it possible for you to "play" the great game of life! I'll explain later!)

What you do not "know" is not "so." Since "you" do not "remember" your future, it has not "happened" to "you" yet! A thing "happens" only when it is "experienced." A thing is "experienced" only when it is "known."

Now let's say you've been blessed with a brief glimpse, a split-second "knowing," of your "future." What's happened is that your Spirit—the nonphysical part of you—has simply sped to another place on the Space-Time Continuum and brought back some residual energy—some images or impressions—of that moment or event.

These you can "feel"—or sometimes another who has developed a metaphysical gift can "feel" or "see" these images and energies that are swirling about you.

If you don't like what you "sense" about your "future," step away from that! Just step away from it! In that instant you change your experience—and everyone of You breathes a sigh of relief!

Wait a minute! Whoaaaa—?

You must know—you are now ready to be told—that you exist at every level of the Space-Time Continuum *simultaneously.*

That is, your soul Always Was, Always Is, and Always Will Be—world without end—amen.

I "exist" more places than one?

Of course! You exist *everywhere*—and at all times!

There is a "me" in the future and a "me" in the past?

Well, "future" and "past" do not exist, as we've just taken pains to understand—but, using those words as you have been using them, yes.

There is more than one of me?

There is *only* one of you, but you are much *larger* than you think!

So when the "me" that exists "now" changes something he doesn't like about his "future," the "me" that exists in the "future" no longer has that as part of his experience?

Essentially yes. The whole mosaic changes. But he never loses the experience he's given himself. He's just relieved and happy that "you" don't have to go through that.

But the "me" in the "past" has yet to "experience" this, so he walks right into it?

In a sense, yes. But, of course, "you" can help "him."

I *can?*

Sure. First, by changing what the "you" in *front* of you experienced, the "you" *behind* you may never *have* to experience it! It is by this device that your soul evolves.

In the same way, the *future you* got help from his *own* future self, thus helping *you* avoid what *he* did not.

Did you follow that?

Yes. And it's intriguing. But now I have another question. What about past lives? If I have always been "me"—in the "past" and in the "future"—how could I have been someone *else*, another person, in a past life?

You are a Divine Being, capable of more than one experience at the same "time"—and able to divide your Self into as many different "selves" as you choose.

You can live the "same life" over and over again, in different ways—as I've just explained. And you can also live different lives at different "times" on the Continuum.

Thus, all the while you're being you, here, now—you can also be, and have been—other "selves" in other "times" and "places."

Good grief—this gets "complicateder" and "complicateder"!

Yes—and we've really only just scratched the surface here.

Just know this: You are a being of Divine Proportion, knowing no limitation. A part of you is choosing to know yourself as your presently-experienced Identity. Yet this is by far not the limit of your Being, although you *think that it is.*

Why?

You *must* think that it is, or you cannot do what you've given yourself this life to do.

And what is that? You've told me before, but tell me again, "here" and "now."

You are using all of Life—all of *many* lives—to *be* and *decide* Who You Really Are; to choose and to create Who You Really Are; to experience and to fulfill your current idea about yourself.

You are in an Eternal Moment of Self creation and Self fulfillment through the process of Self expression.

You have drawn the people, events, and circumstances of your life to you as tools with which to fashion the Grandest Version of the Greatest Vision you ever had about yourself.

This process of creation and recreation is ongoing, never ending, and multi-layered. It is all happening "right now" and on many levels.

In your linear reality you see the experience as one of Past, Present, and Future. You imagine yourself to have one life, or perhaps many, but surely only one *at a time.*

But what if there *were* no "time"? Then you'd be having *all your "lives"* at once!

You *are!*

You are living *this* life, your presently realized life, in your Past, your Present, your Future, all at once! Have you ever had a "strange foreboding" about some future event—so powerful that it made you turn away from it?

In your language you call that premonition. From My viewpoint it is simply an awareness you suddenly have of something you've just experienced in your "future."

Your "future you" is saying, "Hey, this was no fun. Don't *do* this!"

You are also living other lives—what you call "past lives"—right now as well—although you experience them as having been in your "past" (if you experience them at all), and that is just as well. It would be very difficult for you to play this wonderful game of life if you had *full awareness* of what is going on. Even this description offered here cannot give you that. If it did, the "game" would be over! The Process *depends* on the Process being complete, as it is—including your lack of total awareness at this stage.

So bless the Process, and accept it as the greatest gift of the Kindest Creator. Embrace the Process, and move through it with peace and wisdom and joy. Use the Process, and transform it from something you *endure* to something you *engage* as a tool in the creation of the most magnificent experience of All Time: the fulfillment of your Divine Self.

How? How can I best do that?

Do not waste the precious moments of this, your present reality, seeking to unveil all of life's secrets.

Those secrets are secrets for a *reason.* Grant your God the benefit of the doubt. Use your Now Moment for the Highest Purpose—the creation and the expression of Who You Really Are.

Decide Who You Are—Who you *want* to be—and then do everything in your power to *be* that.

Use what I have told you about time as a framework, within your limited understanding, upon which to place the constructions of your Grandest Idea.

If an impression comes to you about the "future," *honor* it. If an idea comes to you about a "past life," see if it has any use for you—don't simply ignore it. Most of all, if a way is made known to you to create, display, express, and experience your Divine Self in ever more glory right here, right now, *follow* that way.

And a way *will* be made known to you, because you have asked. Producing this book is a sign of your asking, for you could not be producing it, right now before your very eyes, without an open mind, an open heart, and a soul which is ready to know.

The same is true of those who are now *reading* it. For *they have created it, too.* How *else* could they now be *experiencing it?*

Everyone is creating everything now being experienced—which is another way of saying that *I* am creating everything now being experienced, for *I am everyone.*

Are you getting the symmetry here? Are you seeing the Perfection?

It is all contained in a single truth:

THERE IS ONLY ONE OF US.

6

Tell me about space.

Space is time . . . demonstrated.

In truth there is no such thing as space—pure, "empty" space, with nothing in it. Everything is *something*. Even the "emptiest" space is filled with vapors so thin, so stretched out over infinite areas, that they seem to not be there.

Then, after the vapors are gone, there is energy. Pure energy. This manifests as vibration. Oscillations. Movements of the All at a particular frequency.

Invisible "energy" is the "space" which holds "matter together."

Once—using your linear time as a model—all the matter in the universe was condensed into a tiny speck. You cannot imagine the denseness of this—but that is because you think that matter as it *now* exists is dense.

Actually, what you now call matter is mostly space. All "solid" objects are 2 percent solid "matter" and 98 percent "air"! The space between the tiniest particles of matter in all objects is enormous. It is something like the distance between heavenly bodies in your night sky. Yet these objects you call *solid*.

At one point the entire universe actually *was* "solid." There was virtually *no space* between the particles of matter. All the matter had the "space" taken out of it—and with the enormous "space" gone, that matter filled an area smaller than the head of a pin.

There was actually a "time" before that "time" when there was no matter at all—just the purest form of Highest Vibration Energy, which you would call *anti-matter*.

This was the time "before" time—before the physical universe as you know it existed. *Nothing* existed as matter. Some people conceive of this as paradise, or "heaven," because "nothing was the matter"!

(It is no accident that today in your language, when you suspect something is wrong, you say, "What's the matter?")

In the beginning, pure energy—*Me!*—vibrated, oscillated, so fast as to form matter—*all the matter of the universe!*

You, too, can perform the same feat. In fact, you *do*, every day. Your *thoughts* are pure vibration—and they can and *do* create physical matter! If enough of you hold the same thought, you can impact, and even create, portions of your physical universe. This was explained to you in detail in *Book 1*.

Is the universe now expanding?

At a rate of speed you cannot imagine!

Will it expand forever?

No. There will come a time when the energies driving the expansion will dissipate, and the energies holding things together will take over—pulling everything "back together" again.

You mean the universe will contract?

Yes. Everything will, quite literally, "fall into place"! And you'll have paradise again. No matter. Pure energy.

In other words—*Me!*

In the end, it'll all come back to Me. That is the origin of your phrase: "It all comes down to this."

That means that we will no longer exist!

Not in physical form. But you will *always exist*. You cannot *not* exist. You *are* that which *Is*.

What will happen after the universe "collapses"?

The whole process will start over again! There will be another so-called Big Bang, and another universe will be born.

It will expand and contract. And then it will do the same thing all over again. And again. And again. Forever and ever. World without end.

This is the breathing in and breathing out of God.

Well, this is all, again, very interesting—but it has very little to do with my everyday life.

As I said before, spending an inordinate amount of time trying to unravel the deepest mysteries of the universe is probably not the most efficient use of your life. Yet there are benefits to be gained from these simple layman's allegories and descriptions of the Larger Process.

Like what?

Like understanding that all things are cyclical—including life itself.

Understanding about the life of the universe will help you to understand about the life of the universe inside *you*.

Life moves in cycles. Everything is cyclical. Everything. When you understand this, you become more able to enjoy the Process—not merely endure it.

All things move cyclically. There is a natural rhythm to life, and everything moves to that rhythm; everything goes with that flow. Thus it is written: "For everything there is a season; and a time for every Purpose under Heaven."

Wise is the one who understands this. Clever is the one who uses it.

Few people understand the rhythms of life more than women. Women live their whole lives by rhythm. They are *in* rhythm with life itself.

Women are more able to "go with the flow" than men. Men want to push, pull, resist, *direct* the flow. Women *experience* it—then mold with it to produce harmony.

A woman hears the melody of flowers in the wind. She sees the beauty of the Unseen. She feels the tugs and pulls and urges of life. She *knows* when it is time to run, and time to rest; time to laugh and time to cry; time to hold on and time to let go.

Most women leave their bodies gracefully. Most men fight the departure. Women treat their bodies more gracefully when they are *in* them, too. Men treat their bodies horribly. That is the same way they treat life.

Of course, there are exceptions to every rule. I'm speaking here in generalities. I'm speaking of how things have been until now. I'm speaking in the broadest terms. But if you look at life, if you admit to yourself what you are seeing, have seen, if you acknowledge what is so, you may find truth in this generality.

Yet that makes me feel sad. That makes me feel as though women are somehow superior beings. That they have more of the "right stuff" than men.

Part of the glorious rhythm of life is the yin and the yang. One Aspect of "Being" is not "more perfect" or "better" than another. Both aspects are simply—and wonderfully—that: aspects.

Men, obviously, embody other reflections of Divinity, which women eye with equal envy.

Yet it has been said that being a man is your testing ground, or your probation. When you have been a man long enough—when you have suffered enough through your own foolishness; when you have inflicted enough pain through the calamities of your own creation; when

you have hurt others enough to stop your own behaviors—
to replace aggression with reason, contempt with compassion, always-winning with no-one-losing—then you may
become a woman.

When you have learned that might is *not* "right"; that
strength is *not* power *over*, but power *with*; that absolute
power demands of others absolutely nothing; when you
understand these things, then you may deserve to wear a
woman's body—for you will at last have understood her
Essence.

Then a woman *is* better than a man.

No! Not "better"—different! It is *you* making that
judgment. There is no such thing as "better" or "worse" in
objective reality. There is only what Is—and what you
wish to Be.

Hot is no better than cold, up no better than down—
a point I have made before. Hence, female is no "better"
than male. It just *is* what it Is. Just as you are what you are.

Yet none of you are restricted, more limited. You can
Be what you wish to Be, choose what you wish to experience. In this lifetime or the next, or the next after that—
just as you did in the lifetime before. Each of you is always
at choice. Each of you is made up of All of It. There is
male and female in each of you. Express and experience
that aspect of you which it pleases you to express and
experience. Yet know that it is *all* open to each of you.

I don't want to get off onto other topics. I want to stay with
this male-female paradigm for a while longer. You promised at
the end of the last book to discuss in much more detail the whole
sexual aspect of this duality.

Yes—I think it is time that we talked, you and I, about
Sex.

7

Why did you create two sexes? Was this the only way you could figure for us to recreate? How should we deal with this incredible experience called sexuality?

Not with shame, that's for sure. And not with guilt, and not with fear.

For shame is not virtue, and guilt is not goodness, and fear is not honor.

And not with lust, for lust is not passion; and not with abandon, for abandon is not freedom; and not with aggressiveness, for aggressiveness is not eagerness.

And, obviously, not with ideas of control or power or domination, for these have nothing to do with Love.

But . . . may sex be used for purposes of simple personal gratification? The surprising answer is yes—because "personal gratification" is just another word for Self Love.

Personal gratification has gotten a bad rap through the years, which is the main reason so much guilt is attached to sex.

You are told you are not to use for personal gratification something which is *intensely personally gratifying!* This obvious contradiction is apparent to you, but you don't know where to go with the conclusion! So you decide that if you feel *guilty* about how good you feel during and after sex, that will at least make it all right.

It's not unlike the famous singer you all know, whom I will not name here, who receives millions of dollars for singing her songs. Asked to comment on her incredible success and the riches it has brought her, she said, "I feel almost *guilty* because I love doing this so much."

The implication is clear. If it's something you love doing, you should not also be rewarded additionally with money. Most people earn money by *doing something they hate*—or something that is at least *hard work*, not *endless joy!*

So the world's message is: If you feel negatively about it, *then you can enjoy it!*

Guilt is often used by you in your attempt to feel *bad* about something you feel *good* about—and thus reconcile yourself with God . . . who you think does not want you to feel good about *anything!*

You are especially not to feel good about joys of the body. And *absolutely* not about (as your grandmother used to whisper) "S-E-X . . ."

Well, the good news is *it's all right to love sex!*

It's also all right to *love your Self!*

In fact, it's mandatory.

What does *not* serve you is to become *addicted* to sex (or anything else). But it *is* "okay" to fall in love with it!

Practice saying this ten times each day:

I LOVE SEX

Practice saying *this* ten times:

I LOVE MONEY

Now, you want a really tough one? Try saying *this* ten times:

I LOVE *ME!*

Here are some other things you are not supposed to love. Practice loving them:

POWER
GLORY
FAME
SUCCESS
WINNING

Want some more? Try *these*. You should *really* feel guilty if you love *these:*

THE ADULATION OF OTHERS
BEING BETTER
HAVING MORE
KNOWING HOW
KNOWING *WHY*

Had enough? Wait! Here's the *ultimate guilt*. You should feel the ultimate guilt if you feel that you:

KNOW GOD

Isn't this interesting? All through your life you have been made to feel guilty about

THE THINGS YOU WANT MOST.

Yet I tell you this: love, love, *love* the things you desire—for your love of them *draws them to you.*

These things are the stuff of life. When you love them, you *love life!* When you declare that you desire them, you announce that you choose all the good that life has to offer!

So choose *sex*—all the sex you can get! And choose *power*—all the power you can muster! And choose *fame*—all the fame you can attain! And choose *success*— all the success you can achieve! And choose *winning*—all the winning you can experience!

Yet do not choose sex instead of love, *but as a celebration of it.* And do not choose power over, *but power with.* And do not choose fame as an end in itself, *but as a means to a larger end.* And do not choose success at the expense of others, *but as a tool with which to assist others.* And do not choose winning at any cost, *but winning that costs others nothing,* and even brings *them gain as well.*

Go ahead and choose the adulation of others—but see all others as beings upon which *you* can shower adulation, and *do* it!

Go ahead and choose being better—but not better than others; rather, better than *you were before*.

Go ahead and choose having more, but only so that you have *more to give*.

And yes, *choose* "knowing how" and "knowing why"—so that you can share all knowledge with others.

And by all means choose to KNOW GOD. In fact, CHOOSE THIS FIRST, and all else will follow.

All of your life you have been taught that it is better to give than to receive. *Yet you cannot give what you do not have.*

This is why self-gratification is so important—and why it is so unfortunate that it has come to sound so ugly.

Obviously, self-gratification at the expense of others is not what we're talking about here. This is not about ignoring the needs of others. Yet life should also not have to be about *ignoring your own needs*.

Give yourself abundant pleasure, and you will have abundant pleasure to give others.

The masters of Tantric sex know this. That's why they encourage masturbation, which some of you actually call a sin.

Masturbation? Oh, boy—You have really stretched the limit here. How can You bring up something like that—how can You even *say* it—in a message that's supposed to be coming from God?

I see. You have a judgment about masturbation.

Well, *I* don't, but a lot of readers might. And I thought You said we were producing this book for others to read.

We are.

Then why are You deliberately offending them?

I am not "deliberately offending" anyone. People are free to be "offended" or not, as they choose. Yet do you really think it is going to be possible for us to candidly and openly talk about human sexuality without *someone* choosing to be "offended"?

No, but there's such a thing as going too far. I don't think most people are ready to hear God talk about masturbation.

If this book is to be limited to what "most people" are ready to hear God talk about, it's going to be a very small book. Most people are never ready to hear what God talks about when God is talking about it. They usually wait 2,000 years.

All right, go ahead. We've all gotten over our initial shock.

Good. I was merely using this life experience (in which you've all engaged, by the way, but of which no one wants to speak) to illustrate a larger point.

The larger point, restated: *Give yourself abundant pleasure, and you will have abundant pleasure to give to others.*

Teachers of what you call Tantric sex—which is a very high form of sexual expression, incidentally—know that if you come to sex with *hunger* for sex, your ability to pleasure your partner and to experience a prolonged and joyful union of souls and bodies—which is a very high reason to experience sexuality, by the way—is greatly diminished.

Tantric lovers, therefore, often self-pleasure before they pleasure each other. This is frequently done in the presence of each other, and usually with the encouragement and help and loving guidance of each other. Then, when initial hungers have been satisfied, the deeper thirst of the two—the thirst for ecstasy through prolonged union—can be gloriously satisfied.

The mutual self-pleasuring is all part of the joyfulness, the playfulness, the lovingness of sexuality fully expressed. It is one of *several* parts. The experience you call coitus, or intercourse, might come at the end of a 2-hour encounter of love. Or it might not. For most of you it is very nearly the *only point* of a 20-minute exercise. That is, 20 minutes if you're lucky!

I had no idea this was going to turn into a sex manual.

It's not. But it wouldn't be so bad if it did. Most people have a lot to learn about sexuality, and its most wondrous, beneficial expression.

I was nevertheless still seeking to illustrate the larger point. The more pleasure you give yourself, the more pleasure you can give to another. Likewise, if you give yourself the pleasure of power, you have more power to share with others. The same is true of fame, wealth, glory, success, or anything else which makes you feel good.

And by the way, I think it's time we looked at why a certain thing *does* make you "feel good."

Okay—I give up. Why?

"Feeling good" is the soul's way of shouting "This is who I am!"

Have you ever been in a classroom where the teacher was taking attendance—calling the roll—and when your name was called you had to say "here"?

Yes.

Well, "feeling good" is the soul's way of saying "here!"

Now a lot of people are ridiculing this whole idea of "doing what feels good." They say this is the road to hell. Yet *I* say it is the road to *heaven!*

Much depends, of course, on what you say "feels good." In other words, what kinds of experiences feel good to you? Yet I tell you this—no kind of evolution ever took place through *denial*. If you are to evolve, it will not be because you've been able to successfully *deny* yourself the things that you *know* "feel good," but because you've *granted* yourself these pleasures—and found something even greater. For how can you know that something is "greater" if you've never tasted the "lesser"?

Religion would have you take its word for it. That is why all religions ultimately fail.

Spirituality, on the other hand, will always succeed.

Religion asks you to learn from the experience of others. Spirituality urges you to seek your own.

Religion cannot stand Spirituality. It cannot abide it. For Spirituality may bring you to a *different conclusion* than a particular religion—and this no known religion can tolerate.

Religion encourages you to explore the thoughts of others and accept them as your own. Spirituality invites you to toss *away* the thoughts of others and come *up* with your own.

"Feeling good" is your way of telling yourself that your last thought was *truth*, that your last word was *wisdom*, that your last action was *love*.

To notice how far you have progressed, to measure how highly you have evolved, simply look to see what makes you "feel good."

Yet don't seek to *force* your evolution—to evolve further, faster—by *denying* what feels good, or stepping away from it.

Self-denial is self-destruction.

Yet also know this—self-regulation is not self-denial. Regulating one's behavior is an *active choice* to do or not do something based on one's decision regarding who they are. If you declare that you are a person who respects the rights of others, a decision not to steal or rob from them, not to rape and plunder, is hardly "self-denial." It is self-*declaration*. That is why it is said that the measure of how far one has evolved is what makes one feel good.

If acting irresponsibly, if behaving in a way which you know might damage others or cause hardship or pain, is what makes you "feel good," then you have not evolved very far.

Awareness is the key here. And it is the task of the elders in your families and communities to create and spread this awareness among the young. It is likewise the job of God's messengers to increase awareness among *all* peoples, so that they may understand that what is done to or for one is done to or for all—because we are all One.

When you come from "we are all One," it is virtually impossible to find that hurting another "feels good." So-called "irresponsible behavior" vanishes. It is within these parameters that evolving beings seek to experience life. It is within these parameters that I say *grant yourself permission* to have *all* that life has to offer—and you will discover it has *more to offer than you've ever imagined*.

You are what you experience. You experience what you express. You express what you have to express. You have what you grant yourself.

I love this—but can we get back to the original question?

Yes. I created two sexes for the same reason I put the "yin" and "yang" in everything—in the whole universe! They are *part* of the yin and the yang, this male and this female. They are the highest living expression of it in your world.

They are the yin and the yang . . . *in form.* In one of *many physical forms.*

The yin and yang, the here and the there . . . the this and the that . . . the up and the down, the hot and the cold, the big and the small, the fast and the slow—the matter and the anti-matter . . .

98

All of it is necessary for you to experience life as you know it.

How may we best express this thing called sexual energy?

Lovingly. Openly.
Playfully. Joyfully.
Outrageously. Passionately. Sacredly. Romantically.
Humorously. Spontaneously. Touchingly. Creatively. Unabashedly. Sensually.
And, of course, Frequently.

There are those who say that the only legitimate purpose of human sexuality is procreation.

Rubbish. Procreation is the happy aftereffect, not the logical forethought, of most human sexual experience. The idea that sex is only to make babies is naive, and the corollary thought that sex should therefore stop when the last child is conceived is worse than naive. It violates human nature—and that is the nature I *gave* you.

Sexual expression is the inevitable result of an eternal process of attraction and rhythmic energy flow which fuels all of life.

I have built into all things an energy that transmits its signal throughout the universe. Every person, animal, plant, rock, tree—*every* physical thing—sends out energy, like a radio transmitter.

You are sending off energy—emitting energy—right now, from the center of your being in all directions. This energy—which is *you*—moves outward in wave patterns. The energy leaves you, moves through walls, over mountains, past the moon, and into Forever. It *never, ever stops.*

Every thought you've ever had colors this energy. (When you think of someone, if that person is sensitive enough, he or she can *feel* it.) Every word you've ever spoken shapes it. Everything you've ever done affects it.

The vibration, the rate of speed, the wavelength, the frequency of your emanations shift and change constantly with your thoughts, moods, feelings, words, and actions.

You've heard the saying "sending off good vibes," and it's true. That's very accurate!

Now, every other person is, naturally, doing the same thing. And so the ether—the "air" between you—is *filled with energy;* a Matrix of intertwining, interwoven personal "vibes" that form a tapestry more complex than you could ever imagine.

This weave is the combined energy field within which you live. It is *powerful,* and affects *everything.* Including *you.*

You then send out newly created "vibes," impacted as you are by the *incoming* vibes to which you are being subjected, and these, in turn, add to and shift the Matrix—which in turn affects the energy field of everybody else, which impacts the *vibes they* send off, which impacts the Matrix—which impacts *you* . . . and so forth.

Now you may think this is all just fanciful illusion—but have you ever walked into a room where the "air was so thick you could cut it with a knife"?

Or have you ever heard of two scientists working on the same problem at the same time—on opposite sides of the globe—each working on the problem without the other's knowledge, and each suddenly coming up with the same solution simultaneously—and *independently?*

These are common occurrences, and some of the more obvious manifestations of The Matrix.

The Matrix—the combined current energy field within any given parameter—is a powerful vibe. It can directly impact, affect, and *create* physical objects and events.

("Wherever two or more are gathered in My name. . . .")

Your popular psychology has termed this energy Matrix the "Collective Consciousness." It can, and does, affect *everything on your planet:* the prospects of war and the chances for peace; geophysical upheaval or a planet becalmed; widespread illness or worldwide wellness.

All is the result of consciousness.

So, too, the more specific events and conditions in your personal life.

That's fascinating, but what does it have to do with sex?

Patience. I'm getting to that.

All the world is exchanging energy all the time.

Your energy is pushing out, touching everything else. Everything and everyone else is touching you. But now an interesting thing happens. At some point midway between you and everything else— those energies *meet*.

To make a more vivid description, let's imagine two people in a room. They are on the far sides of the room from each other. We'll call them Tom and Mary.

Now Tom's personal energy is transmitting signals about Tom in a 360-degree circle out in the universe. Some of that energy wave hits Mary.

Mary, meanwhile, is emitting her own energy—some of which hits Tom.

But these energies meet each other in a way you may not have thought of. They meet *midway between* Tom and Mary.

Here, the energies unite (remember now, these energies are *physical phenomena;* they can be *measured, felt*) and combine to form a new energy unit we'll call "Tomary." It is the energy of Tom and Mary combined.

Tom and Mary could very well call this energy The Body Between Us—for it is just that: a body of energy to which both are connected, which both are feeding the continuing energies which flow to it, and which is *sending energies back* to its two "sponsors" along the thread, or cord, or pipeline that always exists within the Matrix. (Indeed, this "pipeline" *is* the Matrix.)

It is *this* *experience* of "Tomary" which is the *truth* of Tom and Mary. It is *to* this Holy Communion that both are drawn. For they feel, along the pipeline, the sublime joy of the Body Between, of the Joined One, of the Blessed Union.

Tom and Mary, standing off at a distance, can *feel*—in a *physical way*—what is going on in the Matrix. Both are urgently *drawn* toward this experience. They want to move toward each other! At once!

Now their "training" sets in. The world has trained them to slow down, to mistrust the feeling, to guard against "hurt," to hold back.

But the soul . . . wants to know *"Tomary"—now!*

If the two are lucky, they will be free enough to set aside their fears and trust that love is all there is.

They are irrevocably drawn now, these two, to the Body Between Them. TOMARY is *already* being experienced *metaphysically*, and Tom and Mary will want to experience it *physically*. So they'll move closer together. Not to get to each *other*. It looks that way to the casual observer. But they are each trying to get to TOMARY. They are trying to reach that place of Divine Union which *already exists* between them. The place where they already know they are One—and what it is like to *Be* One.

So they move toward this "feeling" they are experiencing, and, as they close the gap between them, as they "shorten the cord," the energy they are both sending to TOMARY travels a shorter distance and is thus more intense.

They move closer still. The shorter the distance, the greater the intensity. They move closer still. Once more the intensity increases.

Now they stand just a few feet apart. The Body Between them is glowing hot. Vibrating with terrific speed. The "connection" to and from TOMARY is thicker, wider, brighter, burning with the transfer of incredible energy. The two are said to be "burning with desire." They *are!*

They move closer still.

Now, they touch.

The sensation is almost unbearable. Exquisite. They feel, at the point of their touch, all the energy of TOMARY—all the compacted, intensely unified substance of their Combined Being.

If you open yourself to your greatest sensitivity, you'll be able to feel this subtle, sublime energy as a tingling when you touch—sometimes the "tingling" will run right *through* you—or as heat at the point of your touch—heat which you may also suddenly feel throughout your body—but concentrated deeply within your lower chakra, or energy center.

It will "burn" there especially intensely—and Tom and Mary will now be said to have the "hots" for each other!

Now the two embrace, and they close the gap even further, with Tom, Mary, and Tomary all filling nearly the same space. Tom and Mary can *feel* Tomary between them—and they want to get even *closer*—to literally *meld* with Tomary. To *become* Tomary in *physical form.*

I have created in the male and female bodies a way to do that. At this moment, Tom and Mary's bodies are ready to do that. Tom's body is now ready to literally *enter* Mary. Mary's body is ready to literally *receive Tom within her.*

The tingling, the burning, is now *beyond* intense. It is . . . indescribable. The two physical bodies join. Tom, Mary, *and* Tomary become *One.* In the *flesh.*

Still the energies flow between them. Urgently. Passionately.

They heave. They move. They can't get enough of each other, can't get close enough together. They strive to get *close. Close. CLOSER.*

They explode—literally—and their entire physical bodies convulse. The vibration sends ripples to their fingertips. In the explosion of their oneness they have known the God and the Goddess, the Alpha and the Omega, the All and the Nothing—the Essence of life—the Experience of That Which Is.

There are physical chemistries as well. The two *have* become One—and a *third* entity often *is* created of the two, in *physical form.*

Thus, an *outpicturing* of TOMARY is created. Flesh of their flesh. Blood of their blood.

They have literally *created life!*

Have I not said that *ye are Gods?*

That is the most beautiful description of human sexuality I have ever heard.

You see beauty where you desire to see it. You see ugliness where you are afraid to see beauty.

It would amaze you to know how many people see what I've just said as ugly.

No, it wouldn't. I've already seen how much fear, *and* ugliness, the world has placed around sex. But You do leave a lot of questions.

I am here to answer them. But allow Me to go on with My narrative just a bit further before you start throwing them at Me.

Yes, *please.*

This . . . *dance* that I've just described, this energy interaction I've explained, is occurring all the time—in and with *everything.*

Your energy—beamed from you like a Golden Light— is interacting constantly with everything and everyone else. The closer you are, the more intense the energy. The further away, the more subtle. Yet you are never totally disconnected from *anything.*

There is a point between You and every other person, place, or thing which exists. It is here that two energies meet, forming a third, much less dense, but no less real, energy unit.

Every*one* and every*thing* on the planet—and in the universe—is emitting energy in every direction. This energy mixes with all other energies, criss-crossing in patterns of complexity beyond the ability of your most powerful computers to analyze.

The criss-crossing, intermingling, intertwining energies racing between everything that you can call physical is what *holds physicality together.*

This is the Matrix, of which I have spoken. It is along this Matrix that you send signals to each other—messages, meanings, healings, and other physical effects—created sometimes by individuals but mostly by mass consciousness.

These innumerable energies are, as I have explained, attracted to each other. This is called the Law of Attraction. In this Law, Like attracts Like.

Like Thoughts attract Like Thoughts along the Matrix—and when enough of these similar energies "clump together," so to speak, their vibrations become heavier, they slow down—and some become Matter.

Thoughts *do* create physical form—and when many people are thinking the *same* thing, there is a very high likelihood their thoughts will form a Reality.

(That is why "We'll pray for you" is such a powerful statement. There are enough testimonies to the effectiveness of unified prayer to fill a book.)

It is also true that un-prayerlike thoughts can create "effects." A worldwide consciousness of fear, for instance, or anger, or lack, or insufficiency, can create that experience—across the globe or within a given locale where those collective ideas are strongest.

The Earth nation you call the United States, for example, has long thought itself to be a nation "under God, indivisible, with liberty and justice for all." It is not a coincidence that this nation rose to become the most prosperous on Earth. It is also not surprising that this nation is gradually losing all that it has worked so hard to create—for this nation seems to have lost its vision.

The terms "under God, indivisible," meant just that—they expressed the Universal Truth of Unity; Oneness: a Matrix very difficult to destroy. But the Matrix has been weakened. Religious freedom has become religious righteousness bordering on religious intolerance. Individual freedom has all but vanished as individual responsibility has disappeared.

The notion of *individual responsibility* has been distorted to mean "every man for himself." This is the new philosophy that imagines itself to be harkening back to the Early American tradition of rugged individualism.

But the original sense of individual responsibility upon which the American vision and the American dream was based found its deepest meaning and its highest expression in the concept of *Brotherly Love*.

What made America great was not that every man struggled for his *own* survival, but that every man accepted individual responsibility for the survival of *all*.

America was a nation that would not turn its back on the hungry, would never say no to the needy, would open its arms to the weary and the homeless, and would share its abundance with the world.

Yet as America became great, Americans became greedy. Not all, but many. And, as time went on, more and more.

As Americans saw how good it was *possible* to have it, they sought to have it even better. Yet there was only one way to have more and more and *more*. Someone else had to have less and less and less.

As greed replaced greatness in the American character, there was less room for compassion for the least among the people. The less fortunate were told it was their "own damned fault" if they didn't have more. After all, America was the Land of Opportunity, was it not? No one *except* the less fortunate found it possible to admit that America's opportunity was limited, *institutionally,* to those already on the inside track. In general, these have not included many minorities, such as those of certain skin color or gender.

Americans became arrogant internationally as well. As millions starved across the globe, Americans threw away enough food each day to feed entire nations. America was generous with some, yes—but increasingly her foreign policy came to be an extension of her own vested interests. America helped others when it served America to do so. (That is, when it served America's power structure, America's richest elite, or the military machine that protected those elite—and their collective assets.)

America's founding ideal—Brotherly Love—had been eroded. Now, any talk of being "your brother's keeper" is met with a new brand of Americanism—a sharp mind toward what it takes to hold on to one's own, and a sharp word to any among the less fortunate who would dare ask for their fair share, for their grievances to be redressed.

Each person *must* take responsibility for herself or himself—that is undeniably true. But America—and your world—can truly work only when every person is willing to stand responsible for *all* of you as a *Whole.*

So Collective Consciousness produces collective results.

Exactly—and this has been demonstrated time and time again throughout all of your recorded history.

The Matrix draws itself into itself—exactly as your scientists describe the so-called Black Hole phenomenon. It pulls like-energy to like-energy, even drawing physical objects toward each other.

Those objects must then repel each other—move *away*—or they will merge forever—in effect, disappearing in their present form and taking on a new form.

All beings of consciousness intuitively know this, so all beings of consciousness *move away* from the Permanent Melding in order to maintain their relationship to all other beings. If they did not, they would meld *into* all other beings, and experience the Oneness Forever.

This is the state from which we have come.

Having moved away from this state, we are constantly re-attracted *to* it.

This ebb and flow, "to and fro" movement is the basic rhythm of the universe, *and everything in it*. This is sex—the Synergistic Energy Exchange.

You are constantly being attracted, compelled toward union with one another (and with all that is in the Matrix), then, at the Moment of Unity, being repelled by conscious choice away from that Unity. Your choice is to remain free of It, so that you can *experience* it. For once you become part of that Unity and *remain* there, you cannot *know* it as Unity, since you no longer know Separation.

Put another way: for God to *know* Itself as the All of It, God must know Itself as *not* the All of It.

In you—and in every other energy unit of the universe—God knows Itself as the *Parts* of *All*—and thus gives Itself the possibility of knowing Itself as the *All in All* in Its Own Experience.

I can only experience what I am by experiencing what I am not. Yet I *am* what I am not—and so you see the Divine Dichotomy. Hence, the statement: I Am that I Am.

Now as I said, this natural ebb and flow, this natural *rhythm* of the universe, typifies all of life—including the very movements that *create* life in your reality.

Toward each other you are compelled, as if by some urgent force, only to pull away and separate, only to urgently push toward each other again, once more to separate, and again to hungrily, passionately, urgently seek total union.

Together-apart, together-apart, together-apart your bodies dance, in a movement so basic, so *instinctual*, that you have very little conscious awareness of deliberate action. At some point you shift into automatic. No one needs to tell your bodies what to do. They simply *do it*—with the urgency of *all of life*.

This is life itself, expressing itself as life itself.

And this is life itself producing *new* life in the bosom of its own experience.

All of life works on such a rhythm; all of life IS the rhythm.

And so, all of life is imbued with the gentle rhythm of God—what you call the cycles of life.

Food grows in such cycles. Seasons come and go. Planets spin and circle. Suns explode and implode, and explode again. Universes breathe in and breathe out. All of it happens, *all* of it, in cycles, in rhythms, in vibrations matching the frequencies of God/Goddess—the All.

For God *is* the All, and the Goddess is *everything,* and there is nothing else that is; and all that *ever* was, is *now,* and ever *shall* be, is your world without end.

Amen.

Forethoughts

CHAPTERS 8—15

Well, that was some chapter there concluding the first third of this book, wasn't it? That has to be the most original and spiritually compelling description of human sexual attraction and human sexual experience that I have ever heard. And . . . the discussions surrounding sexuality are not over.

Is gay sex okay? Is "kinky" sex okay? Is "loveless" sex okay? And what about children and sexuality? At what age should children be introduced to information about sex as a life experience?

These questions and more are tackled in the very next chapter.

Yet this is not even the high point, in my opinion, of what's coming next. . . .

We are now going to tackle some of the most explosive topics relating to the human experience. What is "right" and what is "wrong"? To whom do we owe our highest allegiance? Is it appropriate to put oneself ahead of others?

As with the opening portion of this book, in this middle third, too, are some startlingly incisive statements. This one, for example:

> Putting yourself first does not mean being what you term "selfish"—it means being self-aware.

Well, now, that puts things into an entirely different context, doesn't it?

And that is the intention, of course, of this entire book—and of the whole Conversations with God series, nine texts in all. What is being offered here is a new context, a whole new cultural story, within which to experience what it means to be human.

We're going to look here at what it means to be a three-part being made up of Body, Mind, and Soul. As I said, we're going to expand our discussion of human sexuality. But the real highlight of the middle third of *Book 2* is without any doubt chapter 9—one of the single most talked-about sections in the entire nine-volume Conversations with God series.

More people talk to me at lectures, retreats, and book signings about the statements and ideas in this chapter than in any other section or portion of any other CwG text.

One of the longest chapters in any of the CwG books, chapter 9 contains a deep discussion of the way in which we currently educate our children on this planet—and a series of remarkable suggestions on how we might re-create all of that, producing an entirely new educational environment to replace our present school "systems." The chapter even contains specific curriculum suggestions, laying the basis of an entire educational program and a whole new teaching approach for our offspring.

Nothing has proven to be more exciting or inspiring for parents who have read the CwG material. Out of this single chapter has grown a whole non-profit organization, The School of the New Spirituality (www.SchoolofTheNewSpirituality.com).

Then, in the chapter that follows, this continuing dialogue tackles more controversial topics: politics and governance. The points made here are salient and right on the nose . . . as are the even more controversial statements in chapter 11, which has to do with our whole World Order. And *this* is followed by an intense discussion of *consciousness* and the role it plays in the creation of the world as we know it.

This middle third of *Book 2* may be, in terms of social commentary, the meatiest of *any portion of any text* in the nine-book CwG cosmology.

Upon rereading these extraordinarily "action-packed" chapters, I lit up! I remembered how excited I was when this book first came through me. But what really struck me as I closed this portion of the book is how little has changed . . . as I said earlier, how much work there is left to do if we are to create a new collective experience for humanity and for humanity's children in the years ahead.

I was also inspired. Deeply inspired. I experience *Book 2* to be the most politically and socially inspirational book of all that God has given me, and I just wish that a copy of it could be placed on the shelf of every college library in the world and in the hands of every social studies and political science student in all of those universities, not because I think this book has all the answers . . . but because I think it *asks all the right questions.*

And, as I've said, it is deeply inspirational.

Consider chapter 13. If there is a more inspirational chapter in any book offering political and social commentary from a spiritual point of view, I would like to know what it is.

Now look, I am not bragging here. I did not write those words. I experience that those words came directly to the human race from Divinity Itself. God is telling us in this very special book that we, you and I, can be the source of a New Consciousness on this planet. God is saying that we, you and I, can be an inspiration to the world.

I asked how, and in chapter 13, God gave me a direct answer.

When I reread that chapter, I wept the quiet tears of the re-found. I had found myself again. Now *this is Who I Am,* I said to myself, *and this is Who I Choose to Be.*

I imagine that many of those who read this chapter will feel exactly the same way. Yet here is the question: What are we going to do with all of our conscious awareness? Let it just "sit there" in the deep center of our being, doing nothing, creating nothing, producing nothing, changing nothing? Not even in our own experience?

It's one thing for me to notice that I haven't done very much to change the world, but it's another thing to observe that I haven't done much to change even my own little Self over here. Life for me is pretty much the way it has always been. Sure, there have been some small improvements in my behavior, some not-so-nice ways of being that I have reduced in terms of frequency . . . if not eliminated. But is that it? Is that the sum and substance of all that my conversation with God has produced in terms of practical, daily-life outcomes?

Wow. I begin to see the scope of the struggle. This is the inner struggle that Muslims call *jihad*. This is the struggle between the spiritual side of us and the physical-world side of us that Arjuna plaintively asks Lord Krishna about throughout the Bhagavad Gita. This is what Jesus was speaking of when he came back from praying in the garden only to find his disciples sleeping. "The spirit is willing," he said, "but the flesh is weak."

How do we strengthen the flesh? How do we re-engage the *jihad?* How do we render ourselves victorious in Arjuna's battle, which is our own?

I think we do it first by equipping ourselves with insight and vision, that we may see both the folly of our past and the glory of our future. That is what books such as *Conversations with God* are all about. You are not going to find a book on any shelf anywhere that better serves that agenda.

Then we ask ourselves Hamlet's immortal question: Is it nobler in the mind to suffer the slings and arrows of outrageous fortune or to take arms against a sea of troubles and, by opposing, end them?

Yet by what approach, with what device, would we oppose them? Were we to "take up arms," what shall be those arms? What shall be our weapons?

Words, say I. Ideas. New thoughts to replace the old. New visions to recapture humanity's imagination. R. Buckminster Fuller's observation is so perfect here:

> You never change things by fighting the existing reality. To change something, build a new model that makes the existing model obsolete.

This is a "soft form" of opposition. It is to oppose by opposing nothing. In the wonderful book *Happier Than God* this turnaround is spoken of in this way:

> What you resist persists. That is because, by your continued attention to it in a negative way, you continue to place it there. You cannot resist something that is not there. When you resist something, you *place it there.* By focusing angry or frustrated energy on it, you actually give it more life.
>
> This is why all great masters have urged us to "resist not evil." Do not *fight* that which is opposite to your stated desire or your preferred outcome. Rather, relax into it.
>
> I know that may sound strange, but I promise you, it works. Do not become rigid and tense, ready for a *battle. Never oppose that which opposes you.* Do not OPpose, COMpose.
>
> Do you understand? Remember this little rule always: Do not *oppose, compose.*

Compose your original idea of how you want life to show up. And compose *yourself* while you're at it. Come from a place of relaxed assurance that life is functioning perfectly. Yet do not confuse relaxation with acceptance.

"Resist not evil" does not mean that you should not try to change what it is that you do not choose. Changing something is not resisting something, it is merely choosing again. Change is not resistance, but alteration. To modify is not to resist, but rather, to continue Personal Creation.

Modification *is* creation. Resistance is the *end* of creation. It firmly holds the previous creation in place.

Do you see?

At every moment of difficulty and challenge in your life you have a choice: opposition or composition. To repeat: You can either oppose that which you are experiencing, or compose that which you chose.

Compose what you chose.

(*Happier Than God*, by Neale Donald Walsch; released March, 2008 by Emnin Books; distributed by Hampton Roads Publishing Company.)

So I am ready now, ready to take up the struggle once again by seeing it not as a struggle at all, but as a game . . . as I spoke of earlier.

I want to tell you something honestly now. Years after I began calling all of this a "game," I learned that R. Buckminster Fuller, who I quoted just above, used exactly the same terminology in describing humanity's approach to the problems and challenges of our collective reality.

Medard Gabel, the noted author and speaker who co-founded the World Game Institute with Fuller, said in a copyrighted article on his website:

> In the 1960s Buckminster Fuller proposed a "great logistics game" and "world peace game" (later shortened to simply the "World Game") that was intended to be a tool that would facilitate a comprehensive, anticipatory, design science approach to the problems of the world.
>
> The World Game that Fuller envisioned was to be a place where individuals or teams of people came and competed, or cooperated, to "Make the world work, for 100% of humanity, in the shortest possible time, through spontaneous cooperation, without ecological offense or the disadvantage of anyone."

Medard goes on to tell us, "The logic for the use of the word 'game' in the title is even more instructive. It says a lot about Fuller's approach to governance and social problem-solving. Obviously intended as a very serious tool, Fuller chose to call his vision a 'game' because he wanted it seen as something that was accessible to everyone, not just the elite few in the power structure who thought they were running the show."

Medard Gabel is the former executive director of the World Game Institute, an UN-affiliated NGO. He worked with Buckminster Fuller for twelve years, during which time he learned the power and utility of whole systems thinking, global perspectives, and a good sense of humor. Mr. Gabel has been designing, developing, and delivering experiential educational programs since 1970. He is currently the CEO of BigPictureSmallWorld and BigPicture Consulting and is the author of six books on global problems, resources, and strategies, the global energy situation, the global food situation, the U.S. food system, planning, and multinational corporations. BigPictureSmallWorld may be reached at:

281 Bishop Hollow Road
Media, PA 19063
1.866.820.8133 (toll free in U.S.)
1.610.566.0156
fax 1.610.566.7890
or via e-mail through the website at
http://www.bigpicturesmallworld.com/mg.shtml

Let us, then, join with the great minds of our time in seizing this moment and moving our personal reality forward to include Possibility Thinking and a new willingness to embrace—or at least to discuss—the far-reaching ideas in books such as the one you are holding in your hand.

And if you would like more resources with which to play as you take your place on the team in this "game," you may wish to check out the additional Internet sites below:

www.HumanitysTeam.com
www.barbaramarxhubbard.com
www.jeanhouston.org
www.anhglobal.org
www.nealedonaldwalsch.com

8

The interesting thing about talking with You is that You always leave me with more questions than answers. Now I have questions about politics as well as sex!

Some say they're the same thing, that in politics all you ever do is get—

Wait a minute! You're not going to use an *obscenity*, are You?

Well, yes, I thought I would shock you a little.

Hey, HEY! Cut it *out!* God isn't supposed to talk like that!

Then why do *you?*

Most of us *don't.*

The hell you don't.

Those people who are *God fearing* don't!

Oh, I see, you have to *fear* God in order not to offend Him.

And who says I am *offended,* anyway, by a simple word?

And, finally, don't you find it interesting that a word some of you use in the height of passion to describe great sex, you also use as your highest insult? Does that tell you anything about the way you feel about sexuality?

I think You've gotten confused. I don't think people use that term to describe a glorious, truly romantic sexual moment.

Oh, really? Have you been in any bedrooms lately?

No. Have You?

I am in *all* of them—all the time.

Well, that should make us all feel comfortable.

What? Are you saying that you do things in your bedroom that you wouldn't do in front of God—?

Most people aren't comfortable with *anyone* watching, much less *God*.

Yet in some cultures—Aboriginal, some Polynesian—lovemaking is done quite openly.

Yes, well, most people haven't progressed to that level of freedom. In fact, they would consider such behavior regression—to a primitive, pagan state.

These people you call "pagans" have an enormous respect for life. They know nothing of rape, and there are virtually no killings in their societies. Your society puts sex—a very natural, normal human function—under cover, then turns around and kills people right out in the open. *That* is the obscenity!

You've made sex so dirty, shameful, taboo, that you're embarrassed to do it!

Nonsense. Most people simply have a different—they might even say a higher—sense of propriety about sex. They consider it a private interacting; for some, a sacred part of their relationship.

Lack of privacy does not equal lack of sanctity. Most of humanity's most sacred rites are performed in public.

Do not confuse privacy with sanctity. Most of your *worst* actions are taken in private, and you save only your best behavior for public display.

This is not an argument for public sex; it is merely a noting that privacy does not necessarily equal sanctity—nor does publicity rob you of it.

As for propriety, that single word and the behavioral concept behind it have done more to inhibit men's and women's greatest joys than any other human construction—except the idea that God is punitive—which *finished* the job.

Apparently, you don't believe in propriety.

The trouble with "propriety" is that someone has to set the standards. This means, automatically, that your behaviors are being limited, directed, *dictated* by someone *else's* idea of what should bring you joy.

In matters of sexuality—as in all other matters—this can be more than "limiting"; it can be devastating.

I can think of nothing more sad than a man or woman feeling they'd *like* to experience some things, then holding back because they think that what they've dreamt of, fantasized about, would violate the "Standards of Propriety"!

Mind you, it's not something that *they* wouldn't do—it's just something that violates "propriety."

Not just in matters of sexuality, but in all of life, never, ever, *ever*, fail to do something simply because it might violate someone *else's* standards of propriety.

If I had one bumper sticker on my car, it would read:

VIOLATE PROPRIETY

I would certainly put such a sign in every bedroom.

But our sense of what's "right" and "wrong" is what holds society together. How can we cohabitate if we have no agreement on that?

"Propriety" has nothing to do with your relative values of "rightness" or "wrongness." You might all agree that it's "wrong" to kill a man, but is it "wrong" to run naked in the rain? You might all agree that it's "wrong" to take a neighbor's wife, but is it "wrong" to "take" your own wife—or have your wife "take" you—in a particularly delicious way?

"Propriety" seldom refers to legalistic limitations, but more often to simpler matters of what is deemed "appropriate."

"Appropriate" behavior is not always the behavior that's in what you call your "best interests." It is rarely the behavior that brings you the most joy.

Getting back to sexuality, You're saying, then, that any behavior is acceptable behavior so long as there is mutual consent among all those involved and affected?

Shouldn't that be true of all of life?

But sometimes we don't know who will be affected, or how—

You must be sensitive to that. You must be keenly aware. And where you truly cannot know, and cannot guess, you must err on the side of Love.

The central question in ANY decision is, "What would love do now?"

Love for *yourself,* and love for *all others* who are *affected or involved.*

If you love another, you will not do anything that you believe could or would hurt that person. If there is any question or doubt, you will wait until you can get to clarity on the matter.

But that means others can hold you "hostage." All they have to say is that such and such a thing would "hurt" them, and your actions are restricted.

Only by your Self. Wouldn't you *want* to restrict your own actions to those which do not damage the ones you love?

But what if *you* feel damaged by *not* doing something?

Then you must tell your loved one your truth—that you are feeling hurt, frustrated, reduced by not doing a certain thing; that you would like to do this thing; that you would like your loved one's agreement that you may do it.

You must strive to seek such an agreement. Work to strike a compromise; seek a course of action in which everybody can win.

And if such a course cannot be found?

Then I'll repeat what I have said before:

Betrayal
of yourself
in order not to betray
another
is
Betrayal
nonetheless.
It is the
Highest Betrayal.

Your Shakespeare put this another way:

To thine own Self be true,
and it must follow, as the night the day,
Thou canst not then be false
to any man.

But the man who always "goes with" what he wants becomes a very selfish man. I can't believe You are advocating this.

> You assume that man will always make what you call the "selfish choice." I tell you this: Man *is* capable of making the *highest* choice.
>
> Yet I also tell you this:
>
> The Highest Choice is not *always* the choice which seems to serve another.

In other words, sometimes we must put ourselves first.

> Oh, *always* you must put yourselves first! Then, depending upon what you are trying to do—or what you are seeking to experience—you will make your choice.
>
> When your purpose—your *life* purpose—is very high, so will your choices also be.
>
> Putting yourself first does not mean being what you term "selfish"—it means being self *aware*.

You lay a pretty broad basis for the conduct of human affairs.

> It is only through the exercise of the greatest freedom that the greatest growth is achieved—or even possible.
>
> If all you are doing is following someone *else's* rules, then you have not grown, you have obeyed.
>
> Contrary to your constructions, obedience is not what I want from you. Obedience is not growth, and growth is what I desire.

And if we do not "grow," you throw us in hell, right?

> Wrong. But I have discussed that in *Book 1*, and we'll do so at length in *Book 3*.

Okay. So, within these broad parameters you've laid out, may I ask you some final questions about sex before we leave the subject?

Shoot.

If sex is so wonderful a part of the human experience, why do so many spiritual teachers preach abstinence? And why were so many masters apparently celibate?

For the same reason most of them have been depicted as living simply. Those who evolve to a high level of understanding bring their bodily desires into balance with their minds and souls.

You are three-part beings, and most people experience themselves as a body. Even the mind is forgotten after age 30. No one reads anymore. No one writes. No one teaches. No one learns. The mind is forgotten. It is not nourished. It is not expanded. No new input. The minimum output required. The mind is not fed. It is not awakened. It is lulled, dulled. You do everything you can to disengage it. Television, movies, pulp paperbacks. Whatever you do, don't think, don't think, *don't think!*

So most people live life on a body level. Feed the body, clothe the body, give the body "stuff." Most people haven't read a good book—I mean a book from which they can *learn* something—in years. But they can tell you the entire television schedule for the week. There's something extraordinarily sad in that.

The truth is, most people don't want to have to *think*. They elect leaders, they support governments, they adopt religions requiring *no independent thought.*

"Make it easy for me. Tell me what to do."

Most people want that. Where do I sit? When do I stand? How should I salute? When do I pay? What do you wish me to do?

What are the rules? Where are my boundaries? Tell me, tell me, *tell* me. I'll do it—somebody just *tell* me!

Then they get disgusted, disillusioned. They followed all the rules, they did as they were told. What went wrong? When did it turn sour? Why did it fall apart?

It fell apart the moment you abandoned your mind—the greatest creative tool you ever had.

It's time to make friends with your mind again. Be a companion to it—it's felt so alone. Be a nourisher of it—it's been so starved.

Some of you—a small minority—have understood that you have a body *and* a mind. You've treated your mind well. Still, even among those of you who honor your mind—and things of the mind—few have learned to *use* the mind at more than one-tenth its capacity. If you knew of what your mind is capable, you would never cease to partake of its wonders—and its powers.

And if you think the number of you who balance your life between your body and your mind is small, the number who see yourselves as *three*-part beings—Body, Mind, and Spirit—is minuscule.

Yet you *are* three-part beings. You are more than your body, and more than a body with a mind.

Are you nurturing your soul? Are you even *noticing* it? Are you healing it or hurting it? Are you growing or withering? Are you expanding or contracting?

Is your soul as lonely as your mind? Is it even more neglected? And when was the last time you felt your soul being *expressed*? When was the last time you cried with joy? Wrote poetry? Made music? Danced in the rain? Baked a pie? Painted *anything*? Fixed something that was broken? Kissed a baby? Held a cat to your face? Hiked up a hill? Swam naked? Walked at sunrise? Played the harmonica? Talked 'til dawn? Made love for hours . . . on a beach, in the woods? Communed with nature? Searched for God?

When was the last time you sat alone with the silence, traveling to the deepest part of your being? When was the last time you said hello to your soul?

When you live as a single-faceted creature, you become deeply mired in matters of the body: Money. Sex.

Power. Possessions. Physical stimulations and satisfactions. Security. Fame. Financial gain.

When you live as a dual-faceted creature, you broaden your concerns to include matters of the mind. Companionship; creativity; stimulation of new thoughts, new ideas; creation of new goals, new challenges; personal growth.

When you live as a three-part being, you come at last into balance with yourself. Your concerns include matters of the soul: spiritual identity; life purpose; relationship to God; path of evolution; spiritual growth; ultimate destiny.

As you evolve into higher and higher states of consciousness, you bring into full realization every aspect of your being.

Yet evolution does not mean *dropping* some aspects of Self in favor of others. It simply means expanding focus; turning away from almost exclusive involvement with one aspect, toward genuine love and appreciation for *all* aspects.

Then why do so many teachers espouse complete abstinence from sex?

Because they do not believe that humans can achieve a balance. They believe the sexual energy—and the energies surrounding other worldly experiences—is too powerful to simply moderate; to bring into balance. They believe abstinence is *the only way* to spiritual evolution, rather than merely one possible *result* of it.

Yet isn't it true that some beings who are highly evolved *have* "given up sex"?

Not in the classic sense of the words "to give up." It is not a forced letting go of something you still want but know is "no good to have." It's more of a simple releasing, a movement away from—as one pushes oneself away from the second helping of dessert. Not because the dessert is no good. Not even because it's no good *for* you. But simply because, wonderful as it was, you've had enough.

When you can drop your involvement with sex for that reason, you may want to do so. Then again, you may not. You may never decide that you've "had enough" and may always want this experience, in balance with the other experiences of your Beingness.

That's okay. That's all right. The sexually active are no less qualified for enlightenment, no less spiritually evolved, than the sexually inactive.

What enlightenment and evolution *do* cause you to drop is your *addiction* to sex, your deep *need* to have the experience, your compulsive behaviors.

So, too, your *preoccupation* with money, power, security, possessions, and other experiences of the body will vanish. Yet your genuine *appreciation* for them will not and *should* not. Appreciation for *all* of life is what honors the Process I have created. Disdain for life or any of its joys—even the most basic, physical ones—is disdain for *Me*, the Creator.

For when you call My creation unholy, what do you call Me? Yet when you call My creation sacred, you sanctify your experience of it, and Me as well.

I tell you this: I have created *nothing* disdainful—and, as your Shakespeare said, *nothing* is "evil" lest thinking make it so.

This leads me to some other, final, questions about sex. Is any kind of sex between consenting adults okay?

Yes.

I mean even "kinky" sex? Even loveless sex? Even gay sex?

First, let's be once again clear that nothing is disapproved of by God.

I do not sit here in judgment, calling one action *Good* and another *Evil*.

(As you know, I have discussed this at some length in *Book 1*.)

Now—within the context of what serves you, or disserves you, on your Path of Evolution, only *you* can decide that.

There is a broad-based guideline, however, upon which most evolved souls have agreed.

No action which causes hurt to another leads to rapid evolution.

There is a second guideline as well.

No action involving another may be taken without the other's agreement and permission.

Now let us consider the questions you've just asked within the context of these guidelines.

"Kinky" sex? Well, if it hurts no one, and is done with everyone's permission, what reason would anyone have to call it "wrong"?

Loveless sex? Sex for the "sake of sex" has been debated from the beginning of time. I often think whenever I hear this question that I'd like to go into a roomful of people someday and say, "Everybody here who's never had sex outside of a relationship of deep, lasting, committed, abiding love, raise your hand."

Let me just say this: Loveless *anything* is not the fastest way to the Goddess.

Whether it's loveless sex or loveless spaghetti and meat balls, if you've prepared the feast and are consuming it without love, you're missing the most extraordinary part of the experience.

Is it wrong to miss that? Here again, "wrong" may not be the operative word. "Disadvantageous" would be closer, given that you desire to evolve into a higher spiritual being as rapidly as you can.

Gay sex? So many people want to say that I am against gay sexuality—or the acting out of it. Yet I make no judgment, on this or any other choice you make.

People want to make all kinds of value judgments—about *everything*—and I kind of spoil the party. I won't join them in those judgments, which is especially disconcerting to those who say that *I originated them.*

I do observe this: There was once a time when people thought that marriage between people of differing *races* was not only inadvisable, but *against the law of God.* (Amazingly, some people *still* think this.) They pointed to their Bible as their authority—even as they do for their authority on questions surrounding homosexuality.

You mean it is okay for people of differing races to join together in marriage?

The question is absurd, but not nearly as absurd as some people's certainty that the answer is "no."

Are the questions on homosexuality equally absurd?

You decide. I have no judgment about that, or *anything.* I know you wish that I did. That would make your lives a lot easier. No decisions to make. No tough calls. Everything decided for you. Nothing to do but obey. Not much of a life, at least in terms of creativity or self-empowerment, but what the heck . . . no stress, either.

Let me ask You some questions about sex and children. At what age is it appropriate to allow children to become aware of sexuality as a life experience?

Children are aware of themselves as sexual beings—which is to say, as *human* beings—from the outset of their lives. What many parents on your planet now do is try to discourage them from noticing that. If a baby's hand goes to the "wrong place," you move it away. If a tiny child begins to find moments of self-pleasure in its innocent delight with its own body, you react in horror, and pass that sense of horror on to your child. The child wonders, what did I do, what did I do? Mommy's mad; what did I do?

With your race of beings, it has not been a question of when you introduce your offspring to sex, it has been a question of when you stop demanding that they deny their own identity as sexual beings. Somewhere between the ages of 12 and 17 most of you give up the fight already and say, essentially (although naturally not with words—you don't speak of these things), "Okay, now you can notice that you have sexual parts and sexual things to do with them."

Yet by this time the damage has been done. Your children have been shown for ten years or more that they are to be *ashamed* of those body parts. Some are not even told the proper *name* for them. They hear everything from "wee wee" to "your bottom" to words some of you must strain mightily to invent—all to avoid simply saying "penis" or "vagina."

Having thus gotten very clear that all things having to do with *those* parts of the body are to be hidden, not spoken of, denied, your offspring then explode into puberty not knowing at all what to make of what's going on with them. They've had no preparation at all. Of course, they then act miserable, responding to their newest and most urgent urges awkwardly, if not inappropriately.

This is not necessary, nor do I observe it as serving your offspring, far too many of whom enter their adult lives with sexual taboos, inhibitions, and "hang ups" to beat the band.

Now in enlightened societies offspring are never discouraged, reprimanded, or "corrected" when they begin to find early delight in the nature of their very being. Nor is the sexuality of their parents— that is, the *identity* of their parents as sexual beings—particularly avoided or necessarily hidden. Naked bodies, whether of the parents or the children or their siblings, are seen and treated as being totally natural, totally wonderful, and totally okay—not as things of which to be ashamed.

Sexual functions are also seen and treated as totally natural, totally wonderful, and totally okay.

In some societies, parents couple in full view of their offspring—and what could give children a greater sense of the beauty and the wonder and the pure joy and the total okayness of the sexual expression of love than this? For parents are constantly modeling the "rightness" and "wrongness" of *all* behaviors, and children pick up subtle and not-so-subtle signals from their parents about *everything* through what they see their parents thinking, saying, and doing.

As noted earlier, you may call such societies "pagan" or "primitive," yet it is observable that in such societies rape and crimes of passion are virtually nonexistent, prostitution is laughed at as being absurd, and sexual inhibitions and dysfunctions are unheard of.

While such openness is not recommended just now for your own society (in all but the most extraordinary of settings it would no doubt be far too culturally stigmatizing), it *is* time that the so-called modern civilizations on your planet do something to end the repression, guilt, and shame which too often surrounds and characterizes the totality of your society's sexual expression and experience.

Suggestions? Ideas?

Stop teaching children from the very beginning of their lives that things having to do with the very natural functioning of their bodies are shameful and wrong. Discontinue demonstrating to your offspring that anything sexual is to be hidden. Allow your children to see and observe the romantic side of *you*. Let them see you hugging, touching, gently fondling—let them see that their parents *love each other* and that *showing their love physically* is something that is very natural and very wonderful.

(It would surprise you to know in how many families such a simple lesson has never been taught.)

When your children begin to embrace their own sexual feelings, curiosities and urges, cause them to connect this new and expanding experience of themselves with an inner sense of joy and celebration, not guilt and shame.

And for heaven sake, stop hiding your *bodies* from your children. It's okay if they see you swimming in the nude in a country water hole on a camping trip or in the backyard pool; don't go into apoplexy should they catch a glimpse of you moving from the bedroom to the bathroom without a robe; end this frantic need to cover up, close off, shut down any opportunity, however innocent, for your child to be introduced to you as a being with your own sexual identity. Children think their parents are asexual because their parents have *portrayed themselves that way.* They then imagine that *they* must be this way, because *all children emulate their parents.* (Therapists will tell you that some grown-up offspring have, to this very day, the most difficult time imagining their parents actually "doing it," which, of course, fills these offspring—now patients in the therapist's office—with rage or guilt or shame, because they, naturally, *desire* to "do it," and they can't figure out *what's wrong with them.*)

So talk about sex with your children, laugh about sex with your children, teach them and allow them and remind them and *show them how* to *celebrate* their sexuality. *That* is what you can do for your children. And you do this from the day they are born, with the first kiss, the first hug, the first touch they receive from you, and that they see you receiving from each other.

Thank You. *Thank You.* I was so hoping that You'd bring some *sanity* to this subject. But one final question. When is it appropriate to specifically introduce or discuss or describe sexuality with your children?

They will tell you when that time has come. Each child will make it clear, unmistakably, if you are really watching and listening. It comes in increments, actually. It arrives incrementally. And you will know the age-appropriate way of dealing with the incremental arrival of your child's sexuality if *you* are clear, if you are finished with your own "unfinished business" about all of this.

How do we get to *that* place?

Do what it takes. Enroll in a seminar. See a therapist. Join a group. Read a book. Meditate on it. Discover each other—most of all, discover *each other* as male and female again; discover, revisit, regain, reclaim your *own* sexuality. Celebrate *that*. Enjoy *that*. Own *that*.

Own your own joyful sexuality, and then you can allow and encourage your children to own theirs.

Again, thank You. Now, getting away from the consideration of children and moving back to the larger subject of human sexuality, I have to ask You one more question. And it may seem impertinent and it may seem flippant even, but I can't let this dialogue end without asking it.

Well, stop apologizing and just ask it.

Fine. Is there such a thing as "too much" sex?

No. Of course not. But there is such a thing as too much of a need for sex.

I suggest this:

> *Enjoy everything.*
> *Need nothing.*

Including people?

Including people. *Especially* people. Needing someone is the fastest way to kill a relationship.

But we all like to feel needed.

Then stop it. Like to feel unneeded instead—for the greatest gift you can give someone is the strength and the power *not to need you*, to need you for nothing.

9

Okay, I'm ready to move on. You promised to talk about some of the larger aspects of life on Earth, and ever since your comments about life in the United States I've wanted to talk more about all of this.

> Yes, good. I want *Book 2* to address some of the larger issues facing your planet. And there is no larger issue than the education of your offspring.

We are not doing this well, are we. . . . I can tell by the way You brought that up.

> Well, of course, everything is relative. Relative to what you say you are trying to do, no, you are not doing it well.
>
> Everything I say here, everything I have included in this discussion so far and have caused to be placed in this document, must be put into that context. I am not making judgments of "rightness" or "wrongness," "goodness" or "badness." I simply make observations of your *effectiveness* relative to what you *say you are trying to do.*

I understand that.

> I know you say that you do, but the time may come— even before this dialogue is finished—when you will accuse Me of being judgmental.

I would never accuse You of that. I know better.

> "Knowing better" has not stopped the human race from calling Me a judgmental God in the past.

Well, it will stop me.

We shall see.

You wanted to talk about education.

Indeed. I observe that most of you have misunderstood the meaning, the purpose, and the function of education, to say nothing of the process by which it is best undertaken.

That's a huge statement, and I need some help with it.

Most of the human race has decided that the meaning and the purpose and the function of education is to pass on knowledge; that to educate someone is to give them knowledge—generally, the accumulated knowledge of one's particular family, clan, tribe, society, nation, and world.

Yet education has very little to do with knowledge.

Oh? You could have fooled me.

Clearly.

What does it have to do with then?

Wisdom.

Wisdom.

Yes.

Okay, I give up. What is the difference?

Wisdom is knowledge applied.

So we aren't supposed to try to give our offspring knowledge. We are supposed to try to give our offspring wisdom.

First of all, don't "try" to do anything. *Do it.* Secondly, don't ignore knowledge in favor of wisdom. That would be fatal. On the other hand, don't ignore wisdom in favor of knowledge. That would also be fatal. It would kill education. On your planet, it *is* killing it.

We are ignoring wisdom in favor of knowledge?

In most cases, yes.

How are we doing this?

You are teaching your children what to think instead of how to think.

Explain, please.

Certainly. When you give your children knowledge, you are telling them what to think. That is, you are telling them what they are supposed to know, what you want them to understand is true.

When you give your children wisdom, you do not tell them what to know, or what is true, but, rather, *how to get to their own truth.*

But without knowledge there can be no wisdom.

Agreed. That is why I have said, you cannot ignore knowledge in favor of wisdom. A certain amount of knowledge must be passed on from one generation to the next. Obviously. But as little knowledge as possible. The smaller amount, the better.

Let the child discover for itself. Know this: Knowledge is lost. Wisdom is never forgotten.

So our schools should teach as little as possible?

Your schools should turn their emphasis around. Right now they are focused highly on knowledge, and paying precious little attention to wisdom. Classes in critical thinking, problem solving, and logic are considered by · many parents to be threatening. They want such classes out of the curriculum. As well they might, if they want to protect their way of life. Because children who are allowed to develop their own critical thinking processes are very much likely to *abandon* their parents' morals, standards, and entire way of life.

In order to protect your way of life, you have built an education system based upon the development in the child of memories, not abilities. Children are taught to *remember* facts and fictions—the fictions each society has set up about itself—rather than given the ability to discover and create their own truths.

Programs calling for children to develop *abilities* and *skills* rather than *memories* are soundly ridiculed by those who imagine that they know what a child needs to learn. Yet what you have been teaching your children has led your world *toward* ignorance, not away from it.

Our schools don't teach fictions, they teach facts.

Now you are lying to yourself, just as you lie to your children.

We lie to our children?

Of course you do. Pick up any history book and see. Your histories are written by people who want their children to see the world from a particular point of view. Any attempt to expand historical accounts with a larger view of the facts is sneered at, and called "revisionist." You will not tell the truth about your past to your children, lest they see you for what you really are.

Most history is written from the point of view of that segment of your society you would call white Anglo Saxon Protestant males. When females, or blacks, or others in the minority, say, "Hey, wait a minute. This isn't how it happened. You've left out a huge part here," you cringe and holler and demand that the "revisionists" stop trying to change your textbooks. You don't *want* your children to know how it *really* happened. You want them to know how you *justified* what happened, from your point of view. Shall I give you an example of this?

Please.

In the United States, you do not teach your children everything there is to know about your country's decision to drop atom bombs on two Japanese cities, killing or maiming hundreds of thousands of people. Rather, you give them the facts as you see them—and as you want them to see them.

When an attempt is made to balance this point of view with the point of view of another—in this case, the Japanese—you scream and rage and rant and rave and jump up and down and demand that schools don't *dare* even *think* about presenting such data in their historical review of this important event. Thus you have not taught history at all, but politics.

History is supposed to be an accurate, and full, account of what actually happened. Politics is never about what actually happened. Politics is always one's *point of view* about what happened.

History reveals, politics justifies. History uncovers; tells all. Politics covers; tells only one side.

Politicians hate history truly written. And history, truly written, speaks not so well of politicians, either.

Yet you are wearing the Emperor's New Clothes, for your children ultimately see right through you. Children taught to critically think look at your history and say, "My, how my parents and elders have deluded themselves." This you cannot tolerate, so you drum it out of them. You do not want your children to have the most basic facts. You want them to have *your* take on the facts.

I think you are exaggerating here. I think you've taken this argument a little far.

> Really? Most people in your society do not even want their children to know the most basic facts of *life*. People went bananas when schools simply started teaching children how the human body functions. Now you are not supposed to tell children how AIDS is transmitted, or how to *stop it* from being transmitted. Unless, of course, you tell them from a particular *point of view* how to avoid AIDS. Then it is all right. But simply give them the facts, and let them decide for themselves? Not on your life.

Children are not ready to decide these things for themselves. They have to be properly guided.

> Have you looked at your world lately?

What about it?

> That's how you've guided your children in the past.

No, it's how we *mis*guided them. If the world is in rotten shape today—and in many ways, it is—it is not because we've tried to teach our children the *old* values, but because we've allowed them to be taught all this "new fangled" stuff!

> You really believe that, don't you?

You're damned right, I really believe it! If we'd just kept our children limited to the 3 R's instead of feeding them all this "critical thinking" garbage, we'd be a lot better off today. If we'd kept so-called "sex education" out of the classroom and in the home where it belonged, we wouldn't be seeing teenagers having babies, and single mothers at 17 applying for welfare, and a world run amok. If we'd insisted our young ones live by *our* moral standards, rather than letting them go off and create their own, we wouldn't have turned our once strong, vibrant nation into a pitiable imitation of its former self.

I see.

And one more thing. Don't stand there and tell me how we are supposed to suddenly see ourselves as "wrong" for what we did at Hiroshima and Nagasaki. We *ended the war,* for God's sake. We saved thousands of lives. On *both* sides. It was the price of war. Nobody liked the decision, but it had to be made.

I see.

Yeah, you see. You're just like all the rest of those el pinko liberal Commies. You want us to revise our history, all right. You want us to revise ourselves right out of existence. Then you liberals can have your way at last; take over the world; create your decadent societies; redistribute the wealth. *Power to the people,* and all that crap. Except that's never gotten us anywhere. What we need is a return to the past; to the values of our forefathers. That's what we need!

Done now?

Yeah, I'm done. How did I do?

Pretty good. That was really good.

Well, when you've been around talk radio for a few years, it comes pretty easily.

That is how people on your planet think, isn't it?

You bet it is. And not just in America. I mean, you could change the name of the country, and change the name of the war; insert any offensive military action by any nation at any time in history. Doesn't matter. Everybody thinks they're right. Everyone knows its the *other* person who is wrong. Forget about Hiroshima. Insert Berlin instead. Or Bosnia.

Everybody knows the old values are the ones which worked, too. Everybody knows the world is going to hell. Not just in

America. All over. There is a hue and cry for a return to old values, and for a return to nationalism, everywhere on the planet.

I know that there is.

And what I've done here is try to articulate that feeling, that concern, that outrage.

You did a good job. Almost had Me convinced.

Well? What do you say to those who really do think like this?

I say, do you really think things were better 30 years ago, 40 years ago, 50 years ago? I say memory has poor vision. You remember the good of it, and not the worst of it. It's natural, it's normal. But don't be deceived. Do some *critical thinking*, and not just *memorizing* what others want you to think.

To stay with our example, do you really imagine it was absolutely necessary to drop the atom bomb on Hiroshima? What do your American historians say about the many reports, by those who claim to know more about what really happened, that the Japanese Empire had privately revealed to the United States its willingness to end the war *before* the bomb was dropped? How much of a part did revenge for the horror of Pearl Harbor play in the bombing decision? And, if you accept that dropping the Hiroshima bomb was necessary, why was it necessary to drop a second bomb?

It could be, of course, that your own account of all this is correct. It could be that the American point of view on all this is the way it actually happened. That is not the point of this discussion. The point here is that your educational system does not allow for critical thinking on these issues—or very many other issues, for that matter.

Can you imagine what would happen to a social studies or history teacher in Iowa who asked a class the above questions, inviting and encouraging the students to examine and explore the issues in depth and draw their own conclusions?

That is the point! You don't *want* your young ones drawing their own conclusions. You want them to *come to the same conclusions you came to.* Thus, you doom them to repeat the mistakes to which your conclusions led *you.*

But what about these statements made by so many people about old values and the disintegration of our society today? What about the incredible rise in teen births, or welfare mothers, or our world run amok?

Your world has run amok. On this I will agree. But your world has not run amok because of what you have allowed your schools to teach your children. It has run amok because of what you have not allowed them to teach.

You have not allowed your schools to teach that love is all there is. You have not allowed your schools to speak of a love which is unconditional.

Hell, we won't even allow our *religions* to speak of that.

That's right. And you will not allow your offspring to be taught to celebrate themselves and their bodies, their humanness and their wondrous sexual selves. And you will not allow your children to know that they are, first and foremost, spiritual beings inhabiting a body. Nor do you treat your children as spirits coming into bodies.

In societies where sexuality is openly spoken of, freely discussed, joyously explained and experienced, there is virtually no sexual crime, only a tiny number of births which occur when they are not expected, and no "illegitimate" or unwanted births. In highly evolved societies, *all* births are blessings, and all mothers and all children have their welfare looked after. Indeed, the society would have it no other way.

In societies where history is not bent to the views of the strongest and most powerful, the mistakes of the past are openly acknowledged and never repeated, and *once is enough* for behaviors which are clearly self destructive.

In societies where critical thinking and problem solving and skills for living are taught, rather than facts simply memorized, even so-called "justifiable" actions of the past are held up to intense scrutiny. Nothing is accepted on face value.

How would that work? Let's use our example from World War II. How would a school system teaching life skills, rather than merely facts, approach the historical episode at Hiroshima?

Your teachers would describe to their class exactly what happened there. They would include all the facts—*all* the facts—which led up to that event. They would seek the views of historians from *both* sides of the encounter, realizing that there is more than one point of view on *everything*. They would then not ask the class to memorize the facts of the matter. Instead, they would challenge the class. They would say: "Now, you've heard all about this event. You know all that came before, and all that happened after. We've given you as much of the 'knowledge' of this event as we could get our hands on. Now, from this 'knowledge,' what 'wisdom' comes to you? If you were chosen to solve the problems which were being faced in those days, and which were solved by the dropping of the bomb, how would you solve them? Can you think of a better way?"

Oh, *sure*. That's easy. Anybody can come up with answers *that way*—with the benefit of *hindsight*. Anybody can look over their shoulder and say, "I would have done it differently."

Then why don't you?

I beg your pardon?

I said, then why don't you? Why have you not looked over your shoulder, *learned* from your past, and done it differently? I'll tell you why. Because to allow your children to look at your past and analyze it critically—indeed, to *require* them to do so as a part of their education— would be to run the risk of them *disagreeing* with *how you did things*.

They will disagree anyway, of course. You just won't allow too much of it in your classrooms. So they have to take to the streets. Wave signs. Tear up draft cards. Burn bras and flags. Do whatever they can do to get your attention, to get you to see. Your young people have been screaming at you, "There must be a better way!" Yet you do not hear them. You do not *want* to hear them. And you certainly don't want to encourage them in the *classroom* to start critically thinking about the facts you are giving them.

Just *get it,* you say to them. Don't come in here and tell us we've been doing it wrong. Just *get* that we've been doing it *right*.

That's how you educate your children. That's what you've been calling education.

But there are those who would say it's the young people and their crazy, wacko, liberal ideas, who have taken this country and this world down the tubes. Sent it to hell. Pushed it to the edge of oblivion. Destroyed our values-oriented culture, and replaced it with a do-whatever-you-want-to-do, whatever "feels good," morality which threatens to end our very way of life.

The young people *are* destroying your way of life. The young people have *always* done that. Your job is to encourage it, not discourage it.

It is not your young people who are destroying the rain forests. They are asking you to *stop it.* It is not your young people who are depleting your ozone layer. They are asking you to *stop it*. It is not your young people who are exploiting the poor in sweat shops all over the world. They are asking you to *stop it*. It is not your young people who are taxing you to death, then using the money for war and machines of war. They are asking you to *stop* it. It is not your young people who are ignoring the problems of the weak and the downtrodden, letting hundreds of people die of starvation every day on a planet with more than enough to feed everybody. They are asking you to *stop it*.

It is not your young people who are engaging in the politics of deception and manipulation. They are asking you to *stop it*. It is not your young people who are sexually repressed, ashamed and embarrassed about their own bodies and passing on this shame and embarrassment to their offspring. They are asking you to *stop it*. It is not your young people who have set up a value system which says that "might is right" and a world which solves problems with violence. They are asking you to *stop it*.

Nay, they are not asking you . . . they are *begging you*.

Yet it is young people who are violent! Young people who join gangs and kill each other! Young people who thumb their nose at law and order—at *any* kind of order. Young people who are driving us *crazy!*

When the cries and pleas of young people to change the world are not heard and never heeded; when they see that their cause is lost—that you will have it your way no matter what—young people, who are not stupid, will do the next best thing. If they can't beat you, they will join you.

Your young people have joined you in your behaviors. If they are violent, it is because you are violent. If they are materialistic, it is because you are materialistic. If they are acting crazy, it is because you are acting crazy.

If they are using sex manipulatively, irresponsibly, shamefully, it is because they see you doing the same. The only difference between young people and older people is that young people do what they do out in the open.

Older people hide their behaviors. Older people think that young people cannot see. Yet young people see everything. Nothing is hidden from them. They see the hypocrisy of their elders, and they try desperately to change it. Yet having tried and failed, they see no choice but to imitate it. In this they are wrong, yet they have *never been taught differently.* They have not been allowed to critically analyze what their elders have been doing. They have only been allowed to memorize it.

What you memorize, you memorialize.

How, then, should we educate our young?

First, treat them as spirits. They are spirits, entering a physical body. That is not an easy thing for a spirit to do; not an easy thing for a spirit to get used to. It is very confining, very limiting. So the child will cry out at suddenly being so limited. Hear this cry. Understand it. And give your children as much of a sense of "unlimitedness" as you possibly can.

Next, introduce them to the world you have created with gentleness and care. Be full of care—that is to say, be careful—of what you put into their memory storage units. Children remember everything they see, everything they experience. Why do you spank your children the moment they exit the womb? Do you really imagine this is the only way to get their engines going? Why do you take your babies away from their mothers minutes after they have been separated from the only life-form they have known in all of their present existence? Will not the measuring and the weighing and the prodding and the poking wait for just a moment while the newly born experience the safety and the comfort of that *which has given it life?*

Why do you allow some of the earliest images to which your child is exposed to be images of violence? Who told you this was good for your children? And why do you hide images of love?

Why do you teach your children to be ashamed and embarrassed of their own bodies and their functions by shielding your own body from them, and telling them not to ever touch themselves in ways which pleasure them? What message do you send them about pleasure? And what lessons about the body?

Why do you place your children in schools where competition is allowed and encouraged, where being the "best" and learning the "most" is rewarded, where "performance" is graded, and moving at one's own pace is barely tolerated? What does your child understand from this?

Why do you not teach your children of movement and music and the joy of art and the mystery of fairy tales and the wonder of life? Why do you not bring out what is naturally found *in* the child, rather than seek to put in what is unnatural to the child?

And why do you not allow your young ones to learn logic and critical thinking and problem solving and creation, using the tools of their own intuition and their deepest inner knowing, rather than the rules and the memorized systems and conclusions of a society which has already proven itself to be wholly unable to evolve by these methods, yet continues to use them?

Finally, teach *concepts*, not *subjects*.

Devise a new curriculum, and build it around three Core Concepts:

Awareness

Honesty

Responsibility

Teach your children these concepts from the earliest age. Have them run through the curriculum until the final day. Base your entire educational model upon them. Birth all instruction deep within them.

I don't understand what that would mean.

It means everything you teach would come from within these concepts.

Can you explain that? How would we teach the three R's?

From the earliest primers to your more sophisticated readers, all tales, stories, and subject matter would revolve around the core concepts. That is, they would be stories of awareness, stories dealing with honesty, stories about responsibility. Your children would be introduced to the concepts, injected into the concepts, immersed in the concepts.

Writing tasks likewise would revolve around these Core Concepts, and others which are attendant to them as the child grows in the ability to self express.

Even computation skills would be taught within this framework. Arithmetic and mathematics are not abstractions, but are the most basic tools in the universe for living life. The teaching of all computation skills would be contextualized within the larger life experience in a way which draws attention to, and places focus upon, the Core Concepts and their derivatives.

What are these "derivatives"?

To use a phrase which your media people have made popular, they are the spin-offs. The entire educational model can be based on these spin-offs, replacing the subjects in your present curriculum, which teach, basically, facts.

For instance?

Well, let's use our imagination. What are some of the concepts which are important to you in life?

Uh . . . well, I would say . . . honesty, as you have said.

Yes, go ahead. That's a Core Concept.

And, um . . . fairness. That's an important concept to me.

Good. Any others?

Treating others nicely. That's one. I don't know how to put that into a concept.

Go on. Just let the thoughts flow.

Getting along. Being tolerant. Not hurting others. Seeing others as equal. Those are all things I would hope I could teach my children.

Good. Excellent! Keep going.

Uh . . . believing in yourself. That's a good one. And, uh . . . wait, wait . . . there's one coming. Uh . . . yeah, that's it: walking in dignity. I guess I would call it *walking in dignity*. I don't know how to put that into a better concept, either, but it has to do with the way one carries oneself in one's life, and the way one honors others, and the path others are taking.

This is good stuff. This is all good stuff. You're getting down to it now. And there are many other such concepts which all children must deeply understand if they are to evolve and grow into complete human beings. Yet you do not teach these things in your schools. These are the most important things in life, these things we are now talking of, but you do not teach them in school. You do not teach what it means to be honest. You do not teach what it means to be responsible. You do not teach what it means to be aware of other people's feelings and respectful of other people's paths.

You say it is up to parents to teach these things. Yet parents can only pass on what has been passed on to them. And the sins of the father have been visited upon the son. So you are teaching in your homes the same stuff your parents taught you in their homes.

So? What's wrong with that?

As I keep saying repeatedly here, taken a look at the world lately?

You keep bringing us back to that. You keep making us look at that. But all that isn't our fault. We can't be blamed for the way the rest of the world is.

It is not a question of blame, it is a question of choice. And if you are not responsible for the choices humankind has been making, and *keeps* making, who is?

Well, we can't make ourselves responsible for *all* of it!

I tell you this: Until you are willing to take responsibility for all of it, *you cannot change any of it.*

You cannot keep saying *they* did it, and *they* are doing it, and if only *they* would get it right! Remember the wonderful line from Walt Kelly's comic strip character, Pogo, and never forget it:

"We have met the enemy, and they is us."

We've been repeating the same mistakes for hundreds of years, haven't we. . . .

For thousands of years, my son. You've been making the same mistakes for thousands of years. Humankind has not evolved in its most basic instincts much beyond the caveman era. Yet every attempt to change that is met with scorn. Every challenge to look at your values, and maybe even restructure them, is greeted with fear, and then anger. Now along comes an idea from Me to actually teach higher concepts in *schools*. Oh, boy, now we're really treading on thin ice.

Still, in highly evolved societies, that is exactly what is done.

But the problem is, not all people agree on these concepts, on what they mean. That's why we can't teach them in our schools. Parents go nuts when you try to introduce these things into the curriculum. They say you are teaching "values," and that the school has no place in such instruction.

They are wrong! Again, based on what you say as a race of people that you are trying to do—which is build a better world—they are *wrong*. Schools are *exactly* the place for such instruction. Precisely *because* schools are detached from parents' prejudices. Precisely *because* schools are separated from parents' preconceived notions. You've *seen* what has resulted on your planet from the passing down of values from parent to child. Your planet is a *mess*.

You don't understand the most basic concepts of civilized societies.

You don't know how to solve conflict without violence.

You don't know how to live without fear.

You don't know how to act without self interest.

You don't know how to love without condition.

These are basic—*basic*—understandings, and you have not even begun to approach a full comprehension of them, much less implement them . . . after *thousands and thousands of years.*

Is there any way out of this mess?

Yes! It is in your schools! It is in the education of your young! Your hope is in the next generation, and the next! But you must stop immersing them in the ways of the *past*. Those ways have not worked. They have not taken you where you say you want to go. Yet if you are not careful, you are going to get exactly where you are headed!

So *stop!* Turn around! Sit down together and collect your thoughts. Create the grandest version of the greatest vision you ever had about yourselves as a human race. Then, take the values and concepts which undergird such a vision and *teach them in your schools*.

Why not courses such as . . .

- Understanding Power
- Peaceful Conflict Resolution
- Elements of Loving Relationships
- Personhood and Self Creation
- Body, Mind and Spirit: How They Function
- Engaging Creativity
- Celebrating Self, Valuing Others
- Joyous Sexual Expression
- Fairness
- Tolerance
- Diversities and Similarities
- Ethical Economics
- Creative Consciousness and Mind Power
- Awareness and Wakefulness
- Honesty and Responsibility
- Visibility and Transparency
- Science and Spirituality

Much of this *is* taught right now. We call it Social Studies.

I am not talking about a 2-day unit in a semester-long course. I am talking about *separate courses* on each of these things. I am talking about a complete revision of your schools' curricula. I am speaking of a values-based curriculum. You are now teaching what is largely a facts-based curriculum.

I am talking about focusing your children's attention as much on understanding the core concepts and the theoretical structures around which their value system may be constructed as you now do on dates and facts and statistics.

In the highly evolved societies of your galaxy and your universe (which societies we will be talking about much more specifically in *Book 3*), concepts for living are taught to offspring beginning at a very early age. What you call "facts," which in those societies are considered far less important, are taught at a much later age.

On your planet you have created a society in which little Johnnie has learned how to read before getting out of pre-school, but still hasn't learned how to stop biting his brother. And Susie has perfected her multiplication tables, using flash cards and rote memory, in ever earlier and earlier grades, but has not learned that there is nothing shameful or embarrassing about her body.

Right now your schools exist primarily to provide answers. It would be far more beneficial if their primary function was to ask questions. What does it mean to be honest, or responsible, or "fair"? What are the implications? For that matter, what does it mean that 2+2=4? What are the implications? Highly evolved societies encourage all children to *discover and create those answers for themselves.*

But . . . but, that would lead to *chaos!*

As opposed to the non-chaotic conditions under which you now live your life. . . .

Okay, okay . . . so it would lead to *more* chaos.

I am not suggesting that your schools never share with your offspring any of the things which you have learned or decided about these things. Quite to the contrary. Schools serve their students when they share with Young Ones what Elders have learned and discovered, decided and chosen in the past. Students may then observe how all this has worked. In your schools, however, you present these data to the student as That Which Is Right, when the data really should be offered as simply that: data.

Past Data should not be the basis of Present Truth. Data from a prior time or experience should always and only be the basis for new questions. Always the treasure should be in the question, not in the answer.

And always the questions are the same. With regard to this past data which we have shown you, do you agree, or do you disagree? What do you think? Always, this is the key question. Always this is the focus. What do you think? What do *you* think? *What do you think?*

Now obviously children will bring to this question the values of their parents. Parents will continue to have a strong role—obviously the primary role—in creating the child's system of values. The school's intention and purpose would be to encourage offspring, from the earliest age until the end of formal education, to explore those values, and to learn how to use them, apply them, functionalize them—and yes, even to question them. For parents who do not want children questioning their values are not parents who love their children, but rather, who love themselves *through* their children.

I wish—oh, how I wish—that there were schools such as the ones you describe!

There are some which seek to approach this model.

There are?

> Yes. Read the writings of the man called Rudolph Steiner. Explore the methods of The Waldorf School, which he developed.

Well, of course, I know about those schools. Is this a commercial?

> This is an observation.

Because you knew I was familiar with the Waldorf Schools. You knew that.

> Of course I knew that. Everything in your life has served you, brought you to this moment. I have not just started talking with you at the beginning of this book. I have been talking with you for years, through all of your associations and experiences.

You're saying the Waldorf School is the best?

> No. I am saying it is a model which works, given where you say as a human race you want to go; given what you claim you want to do; given what you say you want to be. I am saying it is an example—one of several I could cite, although on your planet and in your society they are rare—of how education may be accomplished in a way which focuses on "wisdom" more than simply "knowledge."

Well, it is a model I very much approve of. There are many differences between a Waldorf School and other schools. Let me give an example. It is a simple one, but it dramatically illustrates the point.

In the Waldorf School, the teacher moves with the children through all levels of the primary and elementary learning experience. For all those years the children have the same teacher, rather than moving from one person to another. Can you imagine the bond which is formed here? Can you see the value?

The teacher comes to know the child as if it were his or her own. The child moves to a level of trust and love with the teacher which opens doors many traditionally oriented schools never dreamed existed. At the end of those years, the teacher reverts to the first grade, starting over again with another group of children and moving through all the years of the curriculum. A dedicated Waldorf teacher may wind up working with only four or five groups of children in an entire career. But he or she has meant something to those children beyond anything that is possible in a traditional school setting.

This educational model recognizes and announces that the *human relationship*, the *bonding* and the *love* which is shared in such a paradigm is just as important as any *facts* the teacher may impart to the child. It is like home schooling, outside the home.

Yes, it is a good model.

There are other good models?

Yes. You are making some progress on your planet with regard to education, but it is very slow. Even the attempt to place a goals oriented, skill-development-focused curriculum in public schools has met with enormous resistance. People see it as threatening, or ineffective. They want children to learn *facts*. Still, there are some inroads. Yet there is much to be done.

And that is only one area of the human experience which could use some overhauling, given what you say as human beings that you are seeking to be.

Yes, I should imagine the political arena could use some changes, too.

To be sure.

10

I've been waiting for this. This is more of what I assumed You were promising me when You told me that *Book 2* would deal with planetary issues on a global scale. So, can we begin our look at our human politics by my asking you what may seem like an elementary question?

> No questions are undeserving or unworthy. Questions are like people.

Ah, good one. Okay then, let me ask: is it wrong to undertake a foreign policy based on your country's own vested interests?

> No. First, from My standpoint, *nothing* is "wrong." But I understand how you use the term, so I will speak within the context of your vocabulary. I'll use the term "wrong" to mean "that which is not serving you, given who and what you choose to be." This is how I've always used the terms "right" and "wrong" with you; it is always within this context, for, in truth, there is no Right and Wrong.
>
> So, within that context, no, it is not wrong to base foreign policy decisions on vested interest considerations. What is wrong is to pretend that you're not doing so.
>
> This most countries do, of course. They take action— or *fail* to take action—for one set of reasons, then give as a rationale another set of reasons.

Why? Why do countries do that?

> Because governments know that if people understood the real reasons for most foreign policy decisions, the people would not support them.

This is true of governments everywhere. There are very few governments which do not deliberately mislead their people. Deception is part of government, for few people would choose to be governed the way they are governed—few would choose to be governed at all—unless government convinced them that its decisions were for their own good.

This is a hard convincing, for most people plainly see the foolishness in government. So government must lie to at least try to hold the people's loyalty. Government is the perfect portrayer of the accuracy of the axiom that if you lie big enough, long enough, the lie becomes the "truth."

People in power must never let the public know how they came to power—nor all that they've done and are willing to do to stay there.

Truth and politics do not and *cannot* mix because politics is the *art* of saying only what needs to be said—and saying it in just the right way—in order to achieve a desired end.

Not all politics are bad, but the art of politics is a *practical* art. It recognizes with great candor the psychology of most people. It simply notices that most people operate out of self-interest. So politics is the way that people of power seek to convince you that *their* self-interest is *your own*.

Governments understand self-interest. That is why governments are very good at designing programs which *give* things to people.

Originally, governments had very limited functions. Their purpose was simply to "preserve and protect." Then someone added "provide." When governments began to be the people's *provider* as well as the people's protector, governments started *creating* society, rather than preserving it.

But aren't governments simply doing what the people want? Don't governments merely provide the mechanism through

which the people provide for themselves on a societal scale? For instance, in America we place a very high value on the dignity of human life, individual freedom, the importance of opportunity, the sanctity of children. So we've made laws and asked government to create programs to provide income for the elderly, so they can retain their dignity past their earning years; to ensure equal employment and housing opportunities for all people—even those who are different from us, or with whose lifestyle we don't agree; to guarantee, through child labor laws, that a nation's children don't become a nation's slaves, and that no family with children goes without the basics of a life with dignity—food, clothing, shelter.

> Such laws reflect well upon your society. Yet, in providing for people's needs, you must be careful not to rob them of their greatest dignity: the exercise of personal power, individual creativity, and the single-minded ingenuity which allows people to notice that they can provide for themselves. It is a delicate balance which must be struck. You people seem to know only how to go from one extreme to the other. Either you want government to "do it all" for the people, or you want to kill all government programs and erase all government laws tomorrow.

Yes, and the problem is that there are so many who *can't* provide for themselves in a society which gives the best life opportunities routinely to those holding the "right" credentials (or, perhaps, not holding the "wrong" ones); who *can't* provide for themselves in a nation where landlords won't rent to large families, companies won't promote women, justice is too often a product of status, access to preventive health care is limited to those with sufficient income, and where many other discriminations and inequalities exist on a massive scale.

> Governments, then, must replace the conscience of the people?

No. Governments *are* the people's conscience, outspoken. It is through governments that people seek, hope, and determine to correct the ills of society.

That is well said. Yet, I repeat, you must take care not to smother yourself in laws trying to guarantee people a chance to breathe!

You cannot legislate morality. You cannot mandate equality.

What is needed is a *shift* of collective consciousness, not an *enforcer* of collective conscience.

Behavior (and all laws, and all government programs) must spring from Beingness, must be a true reflection of Who You *Are*.

The laws of our society *do* reflect who we are! They say to everyone, "This is how it *is* here in America. This is who Americans *are*."

In the best of cases, perhaps. But more often than not, your laws are the announcements of what those in *power* think you *should* be but are not.

The "elitist few" instruct the "ignorant many" through the law.

Precisely.

What's wrong with that? If there are a few of the brightest and best among us willing to look at the problems of society, of the world, and propose solutions, does that not serve the many?

It depends on the motives of those few. And on their clarity. Generally, nothing serves "the many" more than letting them govern themselves.

Anarchy. It's never worked.

You cannot grow and become great when you are constantly being told what to do by government.

It could be argued that government—by that I mean the law by which we've chosen to govern ourselves—is a reflection of society's greatness (or lack thereof), that great societies pass great laws.

And very few of them. For in great societies, very few laws are *necessary*.

Still, truly lawless societies are primitive societies, where "might is right." Laws are man's attempt to level the playing field; to ensure that what is truly right will prevail, weakness or strength notwithstanding. Without codes of behavior upon which we mutually agree, how could we coexist?

I am not suggesting a world with no codes of behavior, no agreements. I am suggesting that your agreements and codes be based on a higher understanding and a grander definition of self-interest.

What most laws actually *do* say is what the most powerful among you have as their vested interest.

Let's just look at one example. Smoking.

Now the law says you cannot grow and use a certain kind of plant, hemp, because, so government tells you, it is not good for you.

Yet the same government says it is all right to grow and use *another* kind of plant, tobacco, not because *it* is good for you (indeed, the government itself says it is *bad*), but, presumably, because you've always done so.

The real reason that the first plant is outlawed and the second is not has nothing to do with health. It has to do with economics. And that is to say, *power*.

Your laws, therefore, do *not* reflect what your society thinks of itself, and wishes to be—your laws reflect *where the power is*.

No fair. You picked a situation where the contradictions are apparent. Most situations are not like that.

On the contrary. Most *are*.

Then what is the solution?

To have as few laws—which are really limits—as possible.

The reason the first weed is outlawed is only *ostensibly* about health. The *truth* is, the first weed is no more addictive and no more a health risk than cigarettes or alcohol, both of which are *protected* by the law. Why is it then not allowed? Because if it were grown, half the cotton growers, nylon and rayon manufacturers, and timber products people in the world would go out of business.

Hemp happens to be one of the most useful, strongest, toughest, longest-lasting materials on your planet. You cannot produce a better fiber for clothes, a stronger substance for ropes, an easier-to-grow-and-harvest source for pulp. You cut down hundreds of thousands of trees per year to give yourself Sunday papers, so that you can read about the decimation of the world's forests. Hemp could provide you with millions of Sunday papers without cutting down one tree. Indeed, it could substitute for so many resource materials, at one-tenth the cost.

And *that is the catch.* Somebody *loses money* if this miraculous plant—which also has extraordinary medicinal properties, incidentally—is allowed to be grown. And *that* is why marijuana is illegal in your country.

It is the same reason you have taken so long to mass produce electric cars, provide affordable, sensible health care, or use solar heat and solar power in every home.

You've had the wherewithal and the technology to produce *all* of these things for *years.* Why, then, do you not have them? *Look to see who would lose money if you did.* There you will find your answer.

This is the Great Society of which you are so proud? Your "great society" has to be dragged, kicking and screaming, to consider the common good. Whenever common good or collective good is mentioned, everyone yells "communism!" In your society, if providing for the good of the many does not produce a huge profit for someone, the *good of the many is more often than not ignored.*

This is true not only in your country, but also around the world. The basic question facing humankind, therefore, is: Can self-interest ever be replaced by the best interests, the *common* interest, of humankind? If so, how?

In the United States you have tried to provide for the common interest, the best interest, through laws. You have failed miserably. Your nation is the richest, most powerful on the Earth, and it has one of the highest infant mortality rates. Why? Because *poor people* cannot *afford* quality pre-natal and post-natal care—and your society is *profit driven.* I cite this as just one example of your miserable failure. The fact that your babies are dying at a higher rate than most other industrialized nations in the world should bother you. It does not. That says volumes about where your priorities are as a society. Other countries provide for the sick and needy, the elderly and infirm. You provide for the rich and wealthy, the influential and the well-placed. Eighty-five percent of retired Americans *live in poverty.* Many of these older Americans, and most people on low income, use the local hospital emergency room as their "family doctor," seeking medical treatment under only the most dire of circumstances, and receiving virtually no preventive health maintenance care at all.

There's no profit, you see, in people who have little to spend . . . they've worn out their *usefulness* . . .

And this is your *great society*—

You make things sound pretty bad. Yet America has done more for the underprivileged and the unfortunate—both here and abroad—then any other nation on Earth.

America has done much, that is observably true. Yet do you know that as a percentage of its gross national product, the United States provides proportionately less for foreign aid than many much smaller countries? The point is that, before you allow yourself to become too self-congratulatory, perhaps you should look at the world around you. For if this is the best your world can do for the less fortunate, you all have much to learn.

You live in a wasteful, decadent society. You've built into virtually everything you make what your engineers call "planned obsolescence." Cars cost three times as much and last a third as long. Clothes fall apart after the tenth wearing. You put chemicals in your food so they can stay on the shelf longer, even if it means your stay on the planet is shorter. You support, encourage, and enable sports teams to pay obscene salaries for ridiculous efforts, while teachers, ministers, and researchers fighting to find a cure for the diseases which kill you go begging for money. You throw away more food each day in your nation's supermarkets, restaurants, and homes than it would take to feed half the world.

Yet this is not an indictment, merely an observation. And not of the United States alone, for the attitudes that sicken the heart are epidemic around the world.

The underprivileged everywhere must grovel and scrimp to merely stay alive, while the few in power protect *and* increase great hoards of cash, lie on sheets of silk, and each morning twist bathroom fixtures made of gold. And as emaciated children of ribs and skin die in the arms of weeping mothers, their country's "leaders" engage in political corruptions which keep donated food stuffs from reaching the starving masses.

No one seems to have the power to alter these conditions, yet the truth is, power is not the problem. No one seems to have the *will*.

And thus it will always be, so long as no one sees another's plight as his own.

Well, why *don't* we? How can we see these atrocities daily and allow them to continue?

Because you do not *care*. It is a lack of *caring*. The entire planet faces a crisis of consciousness. You must decide whether you simply *care for each other.*

It seems such a pathetic question to have to ask. Why can't we love the members of our own family?

You *do* love the members of your own family. You simply have a very limited view of who your family members *are.*

You do not consider yourself part of the human family, and so the problems of the human family are not your own.

How can the peoples of the Earth change their world view?

That depends on what you want to change it *to.*

How can we eliminate more of the pain, more of the suffering?

By eliminating all separations between you. By constructing a new model of the world. By holding it within the framework of a *new idea.*

Which is?

Which is going to be a radical departure from the present world view.

Presently, you see the world—we're speaking geopolitically now—as a collection of nation states, each sovereign, separate and independent of each other.

The internal problems of these independent nation states are, by and large, not considered the problems of the group as a whole—unless and until they *affect* the group as a whole (or the most powerful members of that group).

The group as a whole reacts to the conditions and problems of individual states based on the vested interests of the larger group. If no one in the larger group has anything to *lose*, conditions in an individual state could go to hell, and no one would much care.

Thousands can starve to death each year, hundreds can die in civil war, despots can pillage the countryside, dictators and their armed thugs can rape, plunder, and murder, regimes can strip the people of basic human rights—and the rest of you will do nothing. It is, you say, an "internal problem."

But, when *your* interests are threatened there, when *your* investments, *your* security, *your* quality of life is on the line, you rally your nation, and try to rally your world behind you, and rush in where angels fear to tread.

You then tell the Big Lie—claiming you are doing what you are doing for humanitarian reasons, to help the oppressed peoples of the world, when the truth is, you are simply protecting your own interests.

The proof of this is that where you do not *have* interests, you do not have concern.

The world's political machinery operates on self-interest. What else is new?

Something will have to be new if you wish your world to change. You must begin to see someone else's interests as your own. This will happen only when you reconstruct your global reality and govern yourselves accordingly.

Are you talking about a one-world government?

I am.

11

You promised that in *Book 2* You would get into larger geopolitical issues facing the planet (as opposed to the basically personal issues addressed in *Book 1*), but I didn't think You would enter into *this* debate!

It is time for the world to stop kidding itself, to wake up, to realize that the *only problem of humanity* is lack of love.

Love breeds tolerance, tolerance breeds peace. Intolerance produces war and looks indifferently upon intolerable conditions.

Love cannot be indifferent. It does not know how.

The fastest way to get to a place of love and concern for all humankind is to see all humankind as your *family*.

The fastest way to see all humankind as your family is to *stop separating yourself*. Each of the nation states now making up your world must *unite*.

We do have the United Nations.

Which has been powerless and impotent. In order for that body to work, it would have to be completely restructured. Not impossible, but perhaps difficult and cumbersome.

Okay—what do You propose?

I don't have a "proposal." I merely offer observations. In this dialogue, you tell me what your new choices are, and I offer observations on ways to manifest that. What is it you now *choose* with regard to the current relationship between people and nations on your planet?

I'll use Your words. If I had my way, I would choose for us "to get to a place of love and concern for all humankind."

Given that choice, I observe that what would work would be the formation of a new world political community, with each nation state having an equal say in the world's affairs, and an equal proportionate share of the world's resources.

It'll never work. The "haves" will never surrender their sovereignty, wealth, and resources to the "have-nots." And, argumentatively, why should they?

Because it is *in their best interest.*

They don't see that—and I'm not sure I do.

If you could add billions of dollars a year to your nation's economy—dollars which could be spent to feed the hungry, clothe the needy, house the poor, bring security to the elderly, provide better health, and produce a dignified standard of living for all—wouldn't that be in your nation's best interest?

Well, in America there are those who would argue that it would help the poor at the expense of the rich and of the middle-income taxpayer. Meanwhile, the country continues to go to hell, crime ravages the nation, inflation robs the people of their life savings, unemployment skyrockets, the government grows bigger and fatter, and in school they're handing out condoms.

You sound like a radio talk show.

Well, these *are* the concerns of many Americans.

Then they are short-sighted. Do you not see that if billions of dollars a year—that's millions a month, hundreds and hundreds of thousands a week, unheard of amounts each *day*—could be sunk back into your system . . . that if you *could* use these monies to feed your hungry, clothe your needy, house your poor, bring security to your elderly, and provide health care and dignity to all . . . the *causes* of *crime* would be lost forever? Do you not see that new jobs would mushroom as dollars were pumped back into your economy? That your own government could even be reduced *because it would have less to do?*

I suppose some of that could happen—I can't imagine government *ever* getting smaller!—but just where are these millions and billions going to come from? Taxes imposed by Your new world government? More taking from those who've "worked to get it" to give to those who won't "stand upon their own two feet" and go after it?

Is that how you frame it?

No, but it is how a great *many* people see it, and I wanted to fairly state their view.

Well, I'd like to talk about that later. Right now I don't want to get off track—but I want to come back to that later.

Great.

But you've asked where these new dollars would come from. Well, they would not have to come from any new taxes imposed by the new world community (although members of the community—individual citizens—would *want*, under an enlightened governance, to send 10 percent of their income to provide for society's needs as a whole). Nor would they come from new taxes imposed by any local government. In fact, some local governments would surely be able to reduce taxes.

All of this—all of these benefits—would result from the simple restructuring of your world view, the simpler reordering of your world political configuration.

How?

The money you save from building defense systems and attack weapons.

Oh, *I* get it! You want us to *close down the military!*

Not just *you. Everybody* in the *world*.

But not close *down* your military, simply reduce it—drastically. Internal order would be your only need. You could strengthen local police—something you say you want to do, but cry each year at budget time that you cannot do—at the same time dramatically reducing your spending on weapons of war and preparations for war; that is, offensive and defensive weapons of mass destruction.

First, I think Your figures exaggerate how much could be saved by doing that. Second, I don't think You'll ever convince people they should give up their ability to defend themselves.

Let's look at the numbers. Presently (it is March 25, 1994, as we write this), the world's governments spend about one trillion dollars a year for military purposes. That's a *million dollars a minute* worldwide.

The nations that are *spending* the most could *redirect* the most to the other priorities mentioned. So larger, richer nations *would* see it in their best interests to do so—*if* they thought it was possible. But larger, richer nations cannot imagine going defenseless, for they fear aggression and attack from the nations which envy them and *want what they have.*

There are two ways to eliminate this threat.

1. Share enough of the world's total wealth and resources with all of the world's people so that no one will want and need what someone else has, and everyone may live in dignity and remove themselves from fear.

2. Create a system for the resolution of differences that eliminates the need for war—and even the possibility *of* it.

The people of the world would probably never do this.

They already have.

They have?

Yes. There is a great experiment now going on in your world in just this sort of political order. That experiment is called the United States of America.

Which You said was failing miserably.

It is. It has very far to go before it could be called a success. (As I promised earlier, I'll talk about this—and the attitudes which are now preventing it—later.) Still, it is the best experiment going.

It is as Winston Churchill said. "Democracy is the worst system," he announced, "except all others."

Your nation was the first to take a loose confederation of individual states and successfully unite them into a cohesive group, each submitting to one central authority.

At the time, none of the states wanted to do this, and each resisted mightily, fearing the loss of its individual greatness and claiming that such a union would not serve its best interests.

It may be instructive to understand just what was going on with these individual states at that time.

While they had joined together in a loose confederation, there was no real U.S. Government, and hence no power to enforce the Articles of Confederation to which the states had agreed.

States were conducting their own foreign affairs, several reaching private agreements on trade and other matters with France, Spain, England, and other countries. States traded with each other as well, and although their Articles of Confederation forbade it, some states added tariffs to the goods shipped in from other states—just as they did for goods from across the ocean! Merchants had no choice but to pay at the harbor if they wanted to buy or sell their goods, there being no central *authority*—although there was a written *agreement* to prohibit such taxing.

The individual states also fought wars with each other. Each state considered its militia a standing army, nine states had their own navies, and "Don't tread on me" could have been the official motto of every state in the Confederation.

Over half of the states were even printing their own money. (Although the Confederation had agreed that doing so would also be illegal!)

In short, your original states, though joined together under the *Articles* of Confederation, were acting *exactly as independent nations do today.*

Although they could see that the agreements of their Confederation (such as the granting to Congress the sole authority to coin money) were not working, they staunchly resisted creating and submitting to a central authority that could *enforce* these agreements and put some teeth into them.

Yet, in time, a few progressive leaders began to prevail. They convinced the rank and file that there was more to be *gained* by creating such a new Federation than they would ever lose.

Merchants would save money and increase profits because individual states could no longer tax each other's goods.

Governments would save money and have more to put into programs and services that truly helped *people* because resources would not have to be used to protect individual states from each other.

The people would have greater security and safety, and greater prosperity, too, by cooperating with, rather than fighting with, each other.

Far from losing their greatness, each state could become greater still.

And that, of course, is exactly what has happened.

The same could be made to happen with the 160 nation states in the world today if *they* were to join together in a United Federation. It could mean an end to war.

How so? There would still be disagreements.

So long as humans remain attached to outer things, that is true. There is a way to truly eliminate war—and *all* experience of unrest and lack of peace—but that is a spiritual solution. We are here exploring a geopolitical one.

Actually, the trick is to *combine the two.* Spiritual truth must be lived in practical life to change everyday experience.

Until this change occurs, there *would* still be disagreements. You are right. Yet there need not be wars. There need not be killing.

Are there wars between California and Oregon over water rights? Between Maryland and Virginia over fishing? Between Wisconsin and Illinois, Ohio and Massachusetts?

No.

And why not? Have not various disputes and differences arisen between them?

Through the years, I suppose so.

You can bet on it. But these individual states have voluntarily agreed—it was a simple, *voluntary agreement*—to abide by certain laws and abide by certain compromises on matters common to them, while retaining the right to pass separate statutes on matters relating to each individually.

And when disputes between states *do* arise, due to differing interpretations of the federal law—or someone simply breaking that law—the matter is taken to a court . . . which has been *granted the authority* (that is, *given* the authority *by the states*) to resolve the dispute.

And, if the current body of law does not provide a precedent or a means by which the matter can be brought through the courts to a *satisfactory* resolution, the states and the people in them send their representatives to a central government to try to create agreement on *new* laws that *will* produce a satisfactory circumstance—or, at the very least, a reasonable compromise.

This is how your federation *works*. A system of laws, a system of courts *empowered* by you to interpret those laws, and a Justice system—backed by armed might, if needed—to enforce the decisions of those courts.

Although no one could argue that the system doesn't need improving, this political concoction has worked for more than 200 years!

There is no reason to doubt that *the same recipe will work between nation states as well.*

If this is so simple, why hasn't it been tried?

It *has*. Your League of Nations was an early attempt. The United Nations is the latest.

Yet one failed and the other has been only minimally effective because—like the 13 States of America's original Confederation—the member nation states (particularly the most powerful) are afraid they have *more to lose than to gain* from the reconfiguration.

That is because the "people of power" are more concerned with holding on to their power than with improving the quality of life for *all* people. The "Haves" *know* that such a World Federation would inevitably produce more for the "have-nots"—but the "haves" believe this would come at *their expense* . . . and they're giving up nothing.

Isn't their fear justified—and is wanting to hold on to what you have so long struggled for unreasonable?

First, it is *not* necessarily true that, to give more to those who now hunger and thirst and live without shelter, others must give up their abundance.

As I have pointed out, all you would have to do is take the $1,000,000,000,000 a year spent annually worldwide for military purposes and shift that to humanitarian purposes, and you will have solved the problem without spending an additional penny or shifting *any* of the wealth from where it now resides to where it does not.

(Of course, it could be argued that those international conglomerates whose profits come from war and tools for war would be "losers"—as would their employees and *all* those whose abundance is derived from the world's conflict consciousness—but perhaps your source of abundance is misplaced. If one has to *depend* on the world living in strife in order for one to survive, perhaps this dependence explains why your world resists *any* attempt to create a structure for lasting peace.)

As for the second part of your question, wanting to hold on to what you have struggled so long to acquire, as an individual or as a nation, is not unreasonable, if you come from an Outside World consciousness.

A what?

If you derive your life's greatest happiness from experiences obtainable only in the Outside World—the physical world outside of yourself—you will *never* want to give up an *ounce* of all that you've piled up, as a person and a nation, to make you happy.

And as long as those who "have not" see their *un*happiness tied to the *lack* of material things, they, too, will get caught in the trap. They will constantly want what you have got, and you will constantly refuse to share it.

That is why I said earlier that there is a way to truly eliminate war—and *all* experience of unrest and lack of peace. But this is a *spiritual* solution.

Ultimately, every geopolitical problem, just as every personal problem, breaks down to a spiritual problem.

All of *life* is spiritual, and therefore all of life's problems are spiritually based—and *spiritually solved*.

Wars are created on your planet because somebody has something that somebody else wants. This is what *causes* someone to *do* something that somebody *else* does not want them to do.

All conflict arises from misplaced desire.

The only peace in all the world that is sustaining is Internal Peace.

Let each person find peace within. When you find peace within, you also find that you can do without.

This means simply that you no longer need the things of your outside world. "Not needing" is a great freedom. It frees you, first, from fear: fear that there is something you won't have; fear that there is something you have that you will lose; and fear that without a certain thing, you won't be happy.

Secondly, "not needing" frees you from anger. *Anger is fear announced.* When you have nothing to fear, you have nothing over which to be angry.

You are not angry when you don't get what you want, because your wanting it was simply a preference, not a necessity. You therefore have no fear associated with the possibility of not getting it. Hence, no anger.

You are not angry when you see others doing what you don't want them to do, because you don't *need* them to do or not do *any* particular thing. Hence, no anger.

You are not angry when someone is unkind, because you have no *need* for them to be kind. You have no anger when someone is unloving, because you have no *need* for them to love you. You have no anger when someone is cruel, or hurtful, or seeks to damage you, for you have no *need* for them to behave any other way, and you are clear that you cannot be damaged.

You do not even have anger should someone seek to take your life, because you do not fear death.

When fear is taken from you, all else can be taken from you and you will not be angry.

You know inwardly, intuitively, that everything you've created can be created again, or—more importantly—that it doesn't matter.

When you find Inner Peace, neither the presence nor the absence of any person, place or thing, condition, circumstance, or situation can be the Creator of your state of mind or the cause of your experience of being.

This does not mean that you reject all things of the body. Far from it. You experience being fully in your body and the *delights* of that, as you never have before.

Yet your involvement with things of the body will be voluntary, not mandatory. You will experience bodily sensations because you *choose* to, not because your are *required* to in order to feel happy or to justify sadness.

This one simple change—seeking and finding peace within—could, were it undertaken by everyone, end all wars, eliminate conflict, prevent injustice, and bring the world to everlasting peace.

There is no other formula necessary, or *possible*. World peace is a personal thing!

What is needed is not a change of circumstance, but a change of consciousness.

How can we find inner peace when we are hungry? Be at a place of serenity when we thirst? Remain calm when we are wet and cold and without shelter? Or avoid anger when our loved ones are dying without cause?

You speak so poetically, but is poetry practical? Does it have anything to say to the mother in Ethiopia who watches her emaciated child die for lack of one slice of bread? The man in Central America who feels a bullet rip his body because he tried to stop an army from taking over his village? And what does your poetry say to the woman in Brooklyn raped eight times by a gang? Or the family of six in Ireland blown away by a terrorist bomb planted in a church on a Sunday morning?

> This is difficult to hear, but I tell you this: There is perfection in everything. Strive to see the perfection. This is the change of consciousness of which I speak.
>
> Need nothing. Desire everything. Choose what shows up.
>
> Feel your feelings. Cry your cries. Laugh your laughs. Honor your truth. Yet when all the emotion is done, be still and know that I am God.
>
> In other words, in the midst of the greatest tragedy, see the glory of the process. Even as you die with a bullet through your chest, even as you are being gang-raped.
>
> Now this sounds like such an impossible thing to do. Yet when you move to God consciousness, you can do it.
>
> You don't *have* to do it, of course. It depends on how you wish to experience the moment.
>
> In a moment of great tragedy, the challenge always is to quiet the mind and move deep within the soul.
>
> *You automatically do this when you have no control over it.*
>
> Have you ever talked with a person who accidentally ran a car off a bridge? Or found himself facing a gun? Or nearly drowned? Often they will tell you that time slowed way down, that they were overcome by a curious calm, that there was no fear at all.

"Fear not, for I am with you." That is what poetry has to say to the person facing tragedy. In your darkest hour, I will be your light. In your blackest moment, I will be your consolation. In your most difficult and trying time, I will be your strength. Therefore, have faith! For I am your shepherd; you shall not want. I will cause you to lie down in green pastures; I will lead you beside still waters.

I will restore your soul, and lead you in the paths of righteousness for My Name's sake.

And yea, though you walk through the valley of the Shadow of Death, you will fear *no* evil; for I am with you. My rod and My staff *will* comfort you.

I am preparing a table before you in the presence of your enemies. I shall anoint your head with oil. Your cup will run over.

Surely, goodness and mercy will follow you all the days of your life, and you will dwell in My house—and in My heart—forever.

12

That's wonderful. What You said there is just wonderful. I wish the world could get that. I wish the world could understand, could believe.

> This book will help that. You are helping that. So you are playing a role, you are doing your part, in raising the Collective Consciousness. That is what all must do.

Yes.

Can we move to a new subject now? I think it's important that we talk about this attitude—this idea of things—which You said a while back that You wanted to fairly present.

The attitude to which I am referring is this attitude, held by many people, that the poor have been given enough; that we must stop taxing the rich—penalizing them, in effect, for working hard and "making it"—to provide even more for the poor.

These people believe that the poor are poor basically because they want to be. Many don't even attempt to pull themselves up. They would rather suckle at the government teat than assume responsibility for themselves.

There are many people who believe that redistribution of the wealth—sharing—is a socialistic evil. They cite the Communist Manifesto—"from each according to his ability, to each according to his need"—as evidence of the satanic origin of the idea of ensuring the basic human dignity of all through the efforts of everyone.

These people believe in "every man for himself." If they are told that this concept is cold and heartless, they take refuge in the statement that opportunity knocks at the door of everyone equally; they claim that no man operates under an inherent disadvantage; that if *they* could "make it," *everybody can*—and if someone doesn't, "it's his own damn fault."

You feel that is an arrogant thought, rooted in ungratefulness.

Yes. But what do You feel?

I have no judgment in the matter. It is simply a thought. There is only one question of any relevance regarding this or any other thought. Does it serve you to hold that? In terms of Who You Are and Who You seek to Be, does that thought serve you?

Looking at the world, that is the question people have to ask. Does it serve us to hold this thought?

I observe this: There *are* people—indeed, entire *groups* of people—who have been *born into* what you call disadvantage. This is observably true.

It is also true that at a very high metaphysical level, no one is "disadvantaged," for each soul creates for itself the exact people, events, and circumstances needed to accomplish what It wishes to accomplish.

You choose everything. Your parents. Your country of birth. All the circumstances surrounding your re-entry.

Similarly, throughout the days and times of your life you continue to choose and to create people, events, and circumstances designed to bring you the exact, right, and perfect opportunities you now desire in order to know yourself as you *truly are*.

In other words, no one is "disadvantaged," given what the *soul* wishes to accomplish. For example, the soul may *wish* to work with a handicapped body or in a repressive society or under enormous political or economic constraints, in order to produce the conditions needed to accomplish what it has set out to do.

So we see that people *do* face "disadvantages" in the *physical* sense, but that these are actually the right and perfect conditions *metaphysically.*

As a practical matter, what does that mean to us? Should we offer help to the "disadvantaged," or simply see that, in truth, they are just where they *want* to be and thus allow them to "work out their own Karma"?

That's a very good—and a very important—question.

Remember first that everything you think, say, and do is a reflection of what you've decided about yourself; a statement of Who You Are; an act of *creation* in your deciding who you want to *be.* I keep returning to that, because that is the only thing you are doing here; that is what you are up to. There is nothing else going on, no other agenda for the soul. You are seeking to be and to experience Who You Really Are—and to create that. You are creating yourself anew in every moment of Now.

Now, within that context, when you come across a person who appears, in relative terms as observed within your world, to be disadvantaged, the first question you have to ask is: Who am I and who do I choose to *be,* in relationship to that?

In other words, the first question when you encounter another in *any* circumstance should always be: What do I want here?

Did you hear that? Your first question, always, must be: What do I want here?—not: What does the other person want here?

That's the most fascinating insight I have ever received about the way to proceed in human relationships. It also runs against everything I've ever been taught.

I know. But the reason your relationships are in such a mess is that you're always trying to figure out what the other person wants and what other *people* want—instead of what *you* truly want. Then you have to decide whether to *give* it to them. And here is how you decide: You decide by taking a look at what you may want from *them.* If there's nothing you think you'll want from them, your first reason for giving them what they want disappears, and so you very seldom do. If, on the other hand, you see that there is something you want or may want from them, then your self-survival mode kicks in, and you try to give them what they want.

Then you resent it—especially if the other person doesn't eventually give you what *you* want.

In this game of *I'll Trade You,* you set up a very delicate balance. You meet my needs and I'll meet yours.

Yet the purpose of all human relationships—relationships between nations as well as relationships between individuals—has nothing to do with any of this. The purpose of your Holy Relationship with every other person, place, or thing is not to figure out what *they* want or need, but what *you* require or desire now in order to *grow*, in order to be Who you *want* to Be.

That is why I *created* Relationship to other things. If it weren't for this, you could have continued to live in a *vacuum*, a void, the Eternal Allness whence you came.

Yet in the Allness you simply *are* and cannot *experience* your "awareness" as *anything in particular* because, in the Allness, there is *nothing you are not.*

So I devised a way for you to create anew, and *Know*, Who You Are *in your experience*. I did this by providing you with:

1. Relativity—a system wherein you could exist as a thing in relationship to something else.

2. Forgetfulness—a process by which you willingly submit to total amnesia, so that you can *not know* that relativity is merely a trick, and that you are All of It.

3. Consciousness—a state of Being in which you grow until you reach full awareness, then becoming a True and Living God, creating and experiencing your own reality,

expanding and exploring that reality, changing and *re-creating* that reality as you stretch your consciousness to new limits—or shall we say, to *no limit*.

In this paradigm, *Consciousness is everything*.

Consciousness—that of which you are truly aware—is the basis of all truth and thus of all true spirituality.

But what is the point of it all? First You make us *forget* Who We Are, so that we can remember Who We Are?

Not quite. So that you can *create* Who You Are and Who You *Want to Be*.

This is the act of God being God. It is Me being Me—through *you!*

This is the point of all life.

Through you, I *experience* being Who and What I Am.

Without you, I could know it, but not experience it.

Knowing and experiencing are two different things. I'll choose experiencing every time.

Indeed, I *do*. Through *you*.

I seem to have lost the original question here.

Well, it's hard to keep God on one subject. I'm kind of expansive.

Let's see if we can get back.

Oh, yes—what to do about the less fortunate.

First, decide Who and What You Are in Relationship to them.

Second, if you decide you wish to experience yourself as being Succor, as being Help, as being Love and Compassion and Caring, then look to see how you can *best be those things*.

And notice that your ability to be those things *has nothing to do with what others are being or doing*.

Sometimes the best way to love someone, and the most help you can give, is to *leave them alone* or empower them to help themselves.

It is like a feast. Life is a smorgasbord, and you can give them a *big helping* of *themselves.*

Remember that the greatest help you can give a person is to *wake them up,* to remind them of Who They Really Are. There are many ways to do this. Sometimes with a little bit of help; a push, a shove, a nudge . . . and sometimes with a decision to let them run their course, follow their path, walk their walk, without any interference or intervention from you. (All parents know about this choice and agonize over it daily.)

What you have the opportunity to do for the less fortunate is to re-*mind* them. That is, cause them to be of a New Mind about themselves.

And you, too, have to be of a New Mind about them, for if *you* see them as unfortunate, *they* will.

Jesus' great gift was that he saw everyone as who they truly are. He refused to accept appearances; he refused to believe what others believed of themselves. He always had a higher thought, and he always invited others *to* it.

Yet he also honored where others chose to be. He did not require them to accept his higher idea, merely held it out as an invitation.

He dealt, too, with compassion—and if others chose to see themselves as Beings needing assistance, he did not reject them for their faulty assessment, but allowed them to love their Reality—and lovingly assisted them in playing out their choice.

For Jesus knew that for some the fastest path to Who They Are was the path *through* Who They Are Not.

He did not call this an imperfect path and thus condemn it. Rather he saw this, *too,* as "perfect"—and thus supported everyone in being just who they wanted to be.

Anyone, therefore, who asked Jesus for help received it.

He denied no one—but was always careful to see that the help he gave supported a person's full and honest desire.

If others genuinely sought enlightenment, honestly expressing readiness to move to the next level, Jesus gave them the strength, the courage, the wisdom to do so. He held himself out—and rightly so—as an example and encouraged people, if they could do nothing else, to have faith in *him*. He would not, he said, lead them astray.

Many did put their faith in him—and to this day he helps those who call upon his name. For his soul is committed to waking up those who seek to be fully awake and fully alive in Me.

Yet Christ had *mercy* on those who did not. He therefore rejected self-righteousness and—as does his Father in heaven—made no judgments, ever.

Jesus' idea of Perfect Love was to grant all persons exactly the help they requested, after telling them the kind of help they could *get*.

He never refused to help anyone, and least of all would he do so out of a thought that "you made your bed, now lie in it."

Jesus knew that if he gave people the help they asked for, rather than merely the help he wanted to give, that he was empowering them *at the level at which they were ready to receive empowerment.*

This is the way of all great masters. Those who have walked your planet in the past, and those who are walking it now.

Now I am confused. When is it *dis*empowering to offer help? When does it work against, rather than for, another's growth?

When your help is offered in such a way that it creates continued dependence, rather than rapid independence.

When you allow another, in the name of compassion, to begin to rely on you rather than rely on themselves.

That is not compassion, that is compulsion. You have a power compulsion. Because that sort of helping is really power-tripping. Now this distinction can be very subtle here, and sometimes you don't even know you are power-tripping. You really believe you are simply doing your best to help another . . . yet be careful that you are not simply seeking to create your own self-worth. For to the extent that you allow other persons to make you responsible for them, to that extent you have allowed them to make you powerful. And that, of course, makes you feel worthy.

Yet this kind of help *is an aphrodisiac which seduces the weak.*

The goal is to help the weak grow strong, not to let the weak become weaker.

This is the problem with many government assistance programs, for they often do the latter, rather than the former. Government programs can be self-perpetuating. Their objective can be every bit as much to justify their existence as to help those they are meant to assist.

If there were a limit to all government assistance, people would be helped when they genuinely need help but could not become addicted to that help, substituting *it* for their own self-reliance.

Governments understand that help is power. That is why governments offer as much help to as many people as they can get away with—for the more people government helps, the more people help the government.

Whom the government supports, supports the government.

Then there *should* be no redistribution of wealth. The Communist Manifesto *is* satanic.

Of course, there *is* no Satan, but I understand your meaning.

The idea behind the statement "From each according to his ability, to each according to his need" is not evil, it is beautiful. It is simply another way of saying you are your brother's keeper. It is the implementation of this beautiful idea that can become ugly.

Sharing must be a way of life, not an edict imposed by government. Sharing should be voluntary, not forced.

But—here we go again!—at its best, government *is the people*, and its programs are simply mechanisms by which the people share with many others, as a "way of life." And I would argue that people, collectively through their political systems, have chosen to do so because people have observed, and history has shown, that the "haves" do *not* share with the "have-nots."

The Russian peasant could have waited until hell froze over for the Russian nobility to share its wealth—which was usually gained and enlarged through the hard work of peasants. The peasants were given just enough to subsist on, as the "incentive" to keep working the land—and make the land barons richer. Talk about a *dependency relationship!* This was an I'll-help-you-only-if-you-help-me arrangement more exploitive and more obscene than anything *ever* invented by government!

It was this obscenity against which the Russian peasants revolted. A government which ensured that all people were treated equally was born out of the people's frustration that the "haves" would *not* give to the "have-nots" *of their own accord.*

It was as Marie Antoinette said of the starving masses clamoring beneath her window in rags, while she lounged in a gold inlaid tub on a bejeweled pedestal, munching imported grapes: "Let them eat cake!"

This is the attitude against which the downtrodden have railed. This is the condition causing revolution and creating governments of so-called oppression.

Governments which take from the rich and give to the poor are called oppressive, while governments which do nothing while the rich *exploit* the poor are repressive.

Ask the peasants of Mexico even today. It is said that twenty or thirty families—the rich and powerful elite—literally *run* Mexico (principally because they *own* it!), while twenty or thirty *million* live in utter deprivation. So the peasants in 1993–94 undertook a revolt, seeking to force the elitist government to recognize its duty to help the people provide the means for a life of at least meager dignity. There is a difference between elistist governments and governments "of, by, and for the people."

Are not people's governments created by angry people frustrated over the basic selfishness of human nature? Are not government programs created as a remedy for man's unwillingness to provide a remedy himself?

Is this not the genesis of fair housing laws, child labor statutes, support programs for mothers with dependent children?

Wasn't Social Security government's attempt to provide for older people something that their own families would not or could not provide?

How do we reconcile our hatred of government control with our lack of willingness to do anything we don't *have* to do when there *are* no controls?

It is said that some coal miners worked under *horrible* conditions before governments required the filthy rich mine owners to clean up their filthy mines. Why didn't the owners do so themselves? Because it would have cut into their *profits!* And the rich didn't care how many of the poor *died* in unsafe mines to keep the profits flowing—and growing.

Businesses paid *slave* wages to beginning workers before governments imposed minimum wage requirements. Those who favor going back to the "good old days" say, "So what? They provided *jobs*, didn't they? And who's taking the *risk*, anyway? The worker? No! The *investor*, the *owner*, takes all the risks! So to him should go the biggest reward!"

Anyone who thinks that the workers on whose labors the owners depend should be treated with dignity is called a *communist*.

Anyone who thinks that a person should not be denied housing because of skin color is called a *socialist*.

Anyone who thinks that a woman should not be denied employment opportunities or promotion simply because she's the wrong sex is called a *radical feminist*.

And when governments, through their elected representatives, move to solve these problems that people of power in society steadfastly refuse to solve themselves, those governments are called oppressive! (Never by the people they help, incidentally. Only by the people who refuse to provide the help *themselves*.)

Nowhere is this more evident than in health care. In 1992 an American president and his wife decided it was unfair and inappropriate for millions of Americans to have no access to preventative health care; that notion started a health care debate which catapulted even the medical profession and the insurance industry into the fray.

The real question is not whose solution was better: the plan proposed by the Administration or the plan proposed by private industry. The real question is: *Why didn't private industry propose its own solution long ago?*

I'll *tell* you why. Because it didn't *have to*. No one was complaining. And the industry was driven by profits.

Profits, profits, *profits*.

My point, therefore, is this. We can rail and cry and complain all we want. The plain truth is, governments provide solutions when the private sector won't.

We can also claim that governments are doing what they are doing against the wishes of the people, but so long as people control the government—as they do to a large extent in the United States—the government will continue to produce and require solutions to social ills because the *majority of the people* are *not* rich and powerful, and therefore *legislate for themselves what society will not give them voluntarily*.

Only in countries where the majority of the people do *not* control the government does government do little or nothing about inequities.

So, then, the problem: How much government is too much government? And how much is too little? And where and how do we strike the balance?

Whew! I've never seen you go *on* like this! That's as long as you've held the floor in either of our two books.

Well, you said this book was going to address some of the larger, global problems facing the family of man. I think I've laid out a big one.

Eloquently, yes. Everyone from Toynbee to Jefferson to Marx has been trying to solve it for hundreds of years.

Okay—What's *Your* solution?

We are going to have to go backwards here; we are going to have to go over some old ground.

Go ahead. Maybe I need to hear it twice.

Then we'll start with the fact that I *have* no "solution." And that is because I see none of this as problematical. It just is what it is, and I have no preferences regarding that. I am merely describing here what is observable; what anyone can plainly see.

Okay, You have no solution and You have no preference. Can You offer me an observation?

I observe that the world has yet to come up with a system of government which provides a total solution—although the government in the United States has come the closest so far.

The difficulty is that goodness and fairness are moral issues, not political ones.

Government is the human attempt to mandate goodness and ensure fairness. Yet there is only one place where goodness is born, and that is in the human heart. There is only one place where fairness can be conceptualized, and that is in the human mind. There is only one place where love can be experienced truly, and that is in the human soul. Because the human soul *is love*.

You cannot legislate morality. You cannot pass a law saying "love each other."

We are now going around in circles, as we have covered all of this before. Still, the discussion is good, so keep plugging away at it. Even if we cover the same ground twice or three times, that is okay. The attempt here is to get to the bottom of it; see how you want to create it now.

Well then, I'll ask the same question I asked before. Aren't all laws simply man's attempt to codify moral concepts? Is not "legislation" simply our combined agreement as to what is "right" and "wrong"?

Yes. And certain civil laws—rules and regulations—are required in your primitive society. (You understand that in nonprimitive societies such laws are unnecessary. All beings regulate themselves.) In your society, you are still confronted with some very elementary questions. Shall you stop at the street corner before proceeding? Shall you buy and sell according to certain terms? Will there be any restrictions on how you behave with one another?

But truly, even these basic laws—prohibitions against murdering, damaging, cheating, or even running a red light—shouldn't be needed and *wouldn't* be needed if all people everywhere simply followed the *Laws of Love*.

That is, God's Law.

What is needed is a growth in consciousness, not a growth of government.

You mean if we just followed the Ten Commandments we'd be all right!

There's no such thing as the Ten Commandments. (See *Book 1* for a complete discussion of this.) God's Law is No Law. This is something you cannot understand.

I require nothing.

Many people cannot believe Your last statement.

Have them read *Book 1*. It completely explains this.

Is that what You are suggesting for this world? Complete anarchy?

I am suggesting nothing. I am merely observing what works. I am telling you what is observably so. And no, I do not observe that anarchy—the absence of governance, rules, regulations, or limitations of any kind—would work. Such an arrangement is only practical with advanced beings, which I do not observe human beings to be.

So some level of governance is going to be required until your race evolves to the point where you *naturally do* what is *naturally right*.

You are very wise to govern yourselves in the interim. The points you made a moment ago are salient, unassailable. People often do *not* do what is "right" when left to their own devices.

The real question is not why do governments impose so many rules and regulations on the people, but why do governments *have* to?

The answer has to do with your Separation Consciousness.

The fact that we see ourselves as separate from each other.

Yes.

But if we aren't separate, then we *are* One. And doesn't that mean we *are* responsible for each other?

Yes.

But doesn't that disempower us from achieving individual greatness? If I am responsible for all others, then the Communist Manifesto was right! "From each according to his ability, to each according to his need."

That is, as I've already said, a very noble idea. But it is robbed of its nobility when it is ruthlessly enforced. That was the difficulty with communism. Not the concept, but its implementation.

There are those who say that the concept *had* to be forced because the concept violates the basic nature of man.

You've hit the nail on the head. What needs to be changed is the basic nature of man. That's where the work must be done.

To create the consciousness shift of which You've spoken.

Yes.

But we're going around in circles again. Would not a group consciousness cause individuals to be disempowered?

Let's look at it. If every person on the planet had basic needs met—if the mass of the people could live in dignity and escape the struggle of simple survival—would this not open the way for all of humankind to engage in more noble pursuits?

Would individual greatness really be suppressed if individual survival were guaranteed?

Must universal dignity be sacrificed to individual glory?

What kind of glory is obtained when it is achieved at the expense of another?

I have placed more than sufficient resources on your planet to ensure adequate supplies for all. How can it be that thousands starve to death each year? That hundreds go homeless? That millions cry out for simple dignity?

The kind of help that would end *this* is not the kind of help which disempowers.

If your well-off say they do not want to help the starving and the homeless because they do not want to disempower them, then your well-off are hypocrites. For no one is truly "well off" if they are well off while others are dying.

The evolution of a society is measured by how well it treats the least among its members. As I have said, the challenge is to find the balance between helping people and hurting them.

Any guidelines You can offer?

An overall guideline might be this: When in doubt, always err on the side of compassion.

The test of whether you are helping or hurting: Are your fellow humans enlarged or reduced as a result of your help? Have you made them bigger or smaller? More able or less able?

It has been said that if you give everything to individuals, they will be less willing to work for it themselves.

Yet why should they have to work for the simplest dignity? Is there not enough for all? Why should "working for it" have to do with anything?

Isn't basic human dignity the birthright of every-one? *Oughtn't* it be?

If one seeks *more* than minimum levels—more food, bigger shelters, finer coverings for the body—one can seek to achieve those goals. But ought one have to struggle to even *survive*—on a planet where there is more than enough for everyone?

That is the central question facing humankind.

The challenge is not to make everyone equal, but to give everyone at least the assurance of basic survival with dignity, so that each may then have the chance to choose what more they want from there.

There are those who argue that some don't take that chance even when it is given them.

And they observe correctly. This raises yet another question: to those who don't take the opportunities presented to them, do you owe another chance, and another?

No.

If I took that attitude, you would be lost to hell forever.
I tell you this: Compassion never ends, love never stops, patience never runs out in God's World. Only in the world of man is goodness limited.
In My World, goodness is endless.

Even if we don't deserve it.

You *always* deserve it!

Even if we throw Your goodness back in Your face?

Especially if you do ("If a man slaps you on the right cheek, turn and offer him your left. And if a man asks you to go one mile with him, go with him twain.") When you throw My goodness back in My face (which, by the way, the human race has done to God for millennia), I see that you are merely *mistaken.* You do not know what is in your best interest. I have compassion because your mistake is based not in evil, but in ignorance.

But some people are *basically evil.* Some people are intrinsically bad.

Who told you that?

It is my own observation.

Then you cannot see straight. I have said it to you before: No one does anything evil, given his model of the world.

Put another way, all are doing the best they can at any given moment.

All actions of everyone depend on the data at hand.

I have said before—consciousness is everything. Of what are you aware? What do you know?

But when people attack us, hurt us, damage us, even kill us for their own ends, is that not evil?

I have told you before: *all attack is a call for help.*

No one truly desires to hurt another. Those who do it—including your own governments, by the way—do it out of a misplaced idea that it is the only way to get something they want.

I've already outlined in this book the *higher solution* to this problem. Simply *want nothing*. Have preferences, but no *needs*.

Yet this is a very high state of being; it is the place of Masters.

In terms of geopolitics, why not work together as a world to meet the most basic needs of everyone?

We're doing that—or trying.

After all these thousands of years of human history, that's the most you can say?

The fact is, you have barely evolved at all. You still operate in a primitive "every man for himself" mentality.

You plunder the Earth, rape her of her resources, exploit her people, and systematically disenfranchise those who disagree with you for doing all of this, calling *them* the "radicals."

You do all this for your own selfish purposes, because you've developed a lifestyle that you *cannot maintain any other way.*

You *must* cut down millions of acres of trees each year or you won't be able to have your Sunday paper. You *must* destroy miles of the protective ozone which covers your planet, or you cannot have your hairspray. You *must* pollute your rivers and streams beyond repair or you cannot have your industries to give you Bigger, Better, and More. And you *must* exploit the least among you—the least advantaged, the least educated, the least aware—or you cannot live at the top of the human scale in unheard-of (and unnecessary) luxury. Finally, you must *deny that you are doing this,* or you cannot live with yourself.

You cannot find it in your heart to "live simply, so that others may simply live." That bumper sticker wisdom is too simple for you. It is too much to ask. Too much to give. After all, you've worked so *hard* for what you've got! *You ain't giving up none of it!* And if the rest of the human race—to say nothing of your own children's children—have to suffer for it, tough bananas, right? You did what *you* had to do to survive, to "make it"—they can do the same! After all, it *is* every man for himself, is it not?

Is there any way out of this mess?

Yes. Shall I say it again? A *shift of consciousness.*

You cannot solve the problems which plague humankind through governmental action or by political means. You have been trying that for thousands of years.

The change that must be made can be made only in the hearts of men.

Can You put the change that must be made into one sentence?

I already have several times.

You must stop seeing God as separate from you, and you as separate from each other.

The *only* solution is the Ultimate Truth: nothing exists in the universe that is separate from anything else. *Everything* is intrinsically connected, irrevocably interdependent, interactive, interwoven into the fabric of all of life.

All government, all politics, must be based on this truth. All laws must be rooted in it.

This is the future hope of your race; the only hope for your planet.

How does the Law of Love You spoke of earlier work?

Love gives all and requires nothing.

How can we require nothing?

If everyone in your race gave all, what would you require? The only reason you require *anything* is because someone else is holding back. *Stop holding back!*

This could not work unless we all did it at once.

Indeed, a global consciousness is what is required.

Yet, how will that come about? *Somebody has to start.*

The opportunity is here for you.

You can be the source of this New Consciousness.

You can be the inspiration.

Indeed, you *must* be.

I must?

Who else is there?

13

How can I begin?

Be a light unto the world, and hurt it not. Seek to build, not to destroy.

Bring My people home.

How?

By your shining example. Seek only Godliness. Speak only in truthfulness. Act only in love.

Live the Law of Love now and forevermore. Give everything, require nothing.

Avoid the mundane.

Do not accept the unacceptable.

Teach all who seek to learn of Me.

Make every moment of your life an outpouring of love.

Use every moment to think the highest thought, say the highest word, do the highest deed. In this, glorify your Holy Self, and thus, too, glorify Me.

Bring peace to the Earth by bringing peace to all those whose lives you touch.

Be peace.

Feel and express in every moment your Divine Connection with the All, and with every person, place, and thing.

Embrace every circumstance, own every fault, share every joy, contemplate every mystery, walk in every man's shoes, forgive every offense (including your own), heal every heart, honor every person's truth, adore every person's God, protect every person's rights, preserve every person's dignity, promote every person's interests, provide every person's needs, presume every person's holiness, present every person's greatest gifts, produce every person's blessing, and pronounce every person's future secure in the assured love of God.

Be a living, breathing example of the Highest Truth that resides within you.

Speak humbly of yourself, lest someone mistake your Highest Truth for a boast.

Speak softly, lest someone think you are merely calling for attention.

Speak gently, that all might know of Love.

Speak openly, lest anyone think you have something to hide.

Speak candidly, so you cannot be mistaken.

Speak often, so that your word may truly go forth.

Speak respectfully, that no one be dishonored.

Speak lovingly, that every syllable may heal.

Speak of Me with every utterance.

Make of your life a gift. Remember always, you *are* the gift!

Be a gift to everyone who enters your life, and to everyone whose life you enter. Be careful *not to enter* another's life if you cannot be a gift.

(You can always be a gift, because you always are the gift—yet sometimes you don't let yourself know that.)

When someone enters your life unexpectedly, *look for the gift that person has come to receive from you.*

What an extraordinary way of putting it.

Why else do you think a person has come to you?

I tell you this: *every* person who has ever come to you has come to receive a gift from you. In so doing, he gives a gift *to* you—the gift of your experiencing and fulfilling Who You Are.

When you see this simple truth, when you understand it, you see the greatest truth of all:

I HAVE SENT YOU
NOTHING BUT ANGELS.

14

I am confused. Can we go back just a bit? There seems to be some contradictory data. I felt that You were saying that sometimes the best help we can give people is to leave them alone. Then I felt You were saying, never fail to help someone if you see that person needs help. These two statements seem to be at odds.

Let Me clarify your thinking on this.

Never offer the kind of help that disempowers. Never insist on offering the help you think is needed. Let the person or people in need know all that you have to give—then listen to what they want; see what they are ready to receive.

Offer the help that is wanted. Often, the person or people will say, or exhibit by their behavior, that they just want to be left alone. Despite what *you* think you'd like to give, leaving them alone might be the Highest Gift you can then offer.

If, at a later time, something else is wanted or desired, you will be caused to notice if it is yours to give. If it is, then give it.

Yet strive to give nothing which disempowers. That which disempowers is that which promotes or produces dependency.

In truth, there is *always* some way you can help others which also empowers them.

Completely *ignoring* the plight of another who is truly seeking your help is not the answer, for doing too little no more empowers the other than doing too much. To be of higher consciousness, you may not deliberately ignore the genuine plight of brothers or sisters, claiming that to let them "stew in their own juice" is the highest gift you can give them. That attitude is righteousness and arrogance at the highest level. It merely allows you to justify your non-involvement.

I refer you again to the life of Jesus and to his teachings.

For it was Jesus who told you that I would say to those on My right, Come, you blessed of My children, inherit the kingdom which I have had prepared for you.

For I was hungry and you gave Me to eat; I was thirsty and you gave Me to drink; I was homeless, and you found Me shelter.

I was naked and you clothed Me; I was ill and you visited Me; I was in prison and you brought Me comfort.

And they will say to Me, Lord, when did we see You hungry, and feed You? Or thirsty, and give You drink? And when did we see You homeless and find You shelter? Or naked, and clothe You? And when did we see You ill, or in prison, and comfort You?

And I will answer them, replying:

Verily, verily, I say unto you—inasmuch as you have done it to the least of these, My brethren, so have you done it to Me.

This is My truth, and it still stands for all the ages.

I love You, You know that?

I know you do. And I love you.

Forethoughts

CHAPTERS 16—20

On and on this book plunges into its daring exploration of life as we have been living it on the Earth—and as we could live it if we chose, if we elected to create a new reality, a new world, a new way of being human.

This dialogue pulls no punches, that's for sure. Even today, fifteen years after it was transcribed, many of its thoughts are revolutionary. The last third of this text epitomizes that. It opens with a suggestion that we simply eliminate money. "The simple expedient of uncovering the money trail" would eliminate a huge portion of government and corporate dysfunction in the world, the dialogue asserts. It adds, "The plain fact is that people would never put up with 90 percent of what is going on in the world if they *knew* what was going on."

A new system of funding global services and assistances is also suggested: a voluntary 10 percent deduction from all income, which would be sent to a Worldwide Compensation System. This is more fully described in the pages that follow.

Also discussed is complete visibility and absolute transparency in all affairs, business and personal, as a new way of life on our planet. Then, an unvarnished look (some would say, a *transparent* look) at how we humans are doing presently in creating our society. Touched upon: bias in housing, fistfights in one of the world's legislatures, the problems of the poor, and the opposition of the rich to so much that would heal the world. . . .

Then, this closing section of *Book 2* blows out the walls with a last few big ideas: a top-end limit on the amount of compensation a person can earn and establishment of a One World Government.

So this final third of the text leaps into discussions of many things that some people are not comfortable talking about. Before you turn these last pages, you should know that. It is as I warned at the outset: You may not agree with all of the ideas here, yet the purpose of this book was not to produce *agreement,* but to generate *conversation.* To get us talking again. To get humanity exploring again.

We've been sitting on our hands for a very long time now, convinced that we have come up with, finally but most certainly, the Best Way to Do Things.

One look at the world shows us that, well actually, we have *not* created that, but we're stubborn creatures, you know, and so we continue to *act as if we have.* Worse, any time there is even the quietest, smallest call for change, *we oppose it.* In fact, in many quarters it is not even possible to *talk* about change safely. Simply talking about changing the present world order, changing the present economic system, changing the current political construction, changing standard social mores (much less changing anything at all about our ancient religions), could very quickly get you labeled *persona non grata.*

I think we need more *unwelcome persons* here. On the planet, I mean. In the halls of government, I mean. In the pulpits and at the lecterns and in the newspaper offices and the publishing houses and the network televisions studios. I think we need more *personae non gratae,* or PNG, as they are called in diplomatic circles.

But we need people who are "unwelcome" for the right reasons, people who are unwelcome not because their actions are harmful to others, but because their ideas are harmful to the status quo, threatening to produce a new way of living on our planet. Those threats could ultimately turn into our salvation.

When I finished my reread of *Conversations with God— Book 2*, I realized that this is what the text is all about. It's about ideas that are harmful to the status quo. It's about a new way of being human. It is about exploring topics that we can no longer ignore.

Chapter 16, for instance, opens with a look at what we are doing to our environment. It speaks with crisp clarity here, mincing no words, and I am impressed by the fact that this was written more than a decade before Al Gore rightfully and deservedly made international news with his movie and book, *An Inconvenient Truth*.

My afterthought on this is that we must move, and move now, to stop the ecological degradation of Mother Earth (a living being that many of us call *Gaia*). It is one of the many areas in which those of us in the New Spirituality Movement envision ourselves making a difference.

Turning to some of the other more controversial proposals found in the final third of this book, I completely agree with the elimination of cash as proposed here, and with the idea of a 10 percent across the board flat tax on all earned income credits. You'll want to peruse these sections carefully to see if you agree also. Whether you do or you don't, I think you'll find it interesting reading.

And I whole-*heartedly* agree with the notion of complete visibility and utter transparency in the conduct of our affairs— both business and personal. But I don't want to bamboozle you about that. I don't want you to think that I have practiced that all my life, or even most of my life, because I have not. Throughout most of my younger years I danced around the truth in one way or another, and nearly always when it was important to me to "protect" some aspect of my maneuverings in either my professional or personal life, I simply lied—by commission or omission, by what I said or what I didn't say.

I have really looked at this closely and have seen how out of integrity I have been for so long. It is not a pretty picture. I have not been very happy with myself on this score. And so I have in recent years sought to tell the truth at all times. I address this in my most recent book, which offers 17 steps to being happier than God.

The thirteenth step is . . . "Speak your truth as soon as you know it."

Here is what *Happier Than God* has to say:

> The biggest lesson I have learned in my life revolves around truth. There is no such thing as Absolute Truth in the objective sense, but there is subjective truth, there is *what is true for you,* and that is extraordinarily important in your life.
>
> Seek to live authentically, seek to be fully you, for it is in living with only half of you showing, only half of you known, only half of you expressed, that unhappiness is guaranteed.
>
> Do not hide your personal truth, your authentic feelings, your here-and-now experience from anyone—least of all from your dearest loved ones or your beloved other.
>
> Interestingly, these are often the ones from whom we hide the most. Usually we do it because we do not want to hurt their feelings. Or, perhaps, because we do not want to lose them.
>
> So we keep them in place by keeping them in doubt, by keeping them in the dark,

by not telling them all of what is true for us. This is exactly the opposite of what we most benefit from doing, yet we live as a recluse from the expression of our own truest feelings, hopes, fears, and desires. And that is not living at all, that is dying.

The death is slow, but it is certain. And one morning we wake up and we simply no longer feel alive.

So tell your truth as soon as you know it. Do not think you are saving another person's feelings by holding back or holding in. A wonderful master once taught me: Speak your truth, but soothe your words with peace. You can share the most difficult truth gently. Do so. Do not think that by withholding your truth you are saving others from hurt. You are not. You are killing them softly with your song. And it is disingenuous and dishonest for you to do that.

What I am saying here is that the way to be happier than God is the way of truth. Tell the truth, to everyone about everything, then live your truth, in every moment and in every way, and you will be happy forever in your heart, for truth makes the spirit soar, truth sets the mind free, truth opens the heart, and truth ignites the passion and releases the love of the soul.

I am still not telling my truth in every single instance and every single moment of my life, but I'm getting there—and I am finding that it's really a challenge. I've had to drop my deep aversion to being disapproved of, and I've had to keep searching for ways to say things so they are not uncomfortable for others to hear—or not *as* uncomfortable.

Sometimes it seems like the best thing to do is to say nothing at all, to "let things ride." And, frankly, this makes a certain amount of sense if the matter at hand is something that's just not that important. Just because something is *true* for you does not mean that it has to be spoken. That is not what is meant by transparency. What is meant by visibility and transparency is that one's truth is told when the telling of that truth is important—or when the *not telling of it* would clearly put another at a disadvantage. (You know exactly when that is, by the way. . . .)

So I've learned to place a measuring stick next to every truth that emerges in my mind. "Is this important enough to create possible discomfort?"

Truth almost always creates some level of discomfort—*initially*. It's always *after* the truth is finally spoken that relief sets in. On all sides.

So I have to be ready to create, perhaps, some little discomfort. And I have had to learn to include myself in this equation. That's something I'd not done in the past. I have been willing to experience my own discomfort to no end rather than produce the slightest discomfort in another. But what I discovered is that this can plant the seeds of a greater discontent and sometimes even lead to resentment—which, if I am not careful, can even lead to anger—all over something that might have been resolved so much more easily at the "small discomfort level."

Now I have that single sentence from *Happier Than God* running across my computer monitor as a screen saver:

Tell the truth as soon as you know it.

(A wonderful book on this topic has been written by Dr. Brad Blanton, and I highly recommend it. It's called *Radical Honesty*. I believe it's the very best book available on this subject.)

Moving on . . . nearly all of the observations in the first half of chapter 19 make me angry, or at the very least, frustrated. I just keep thinking, how can human beings go on like this? How can any civilized society keep allowing such things to occur? Can we not see ourselves? Or, worse yet, do we see ourselves and simply not care?

The questions raised in this chapter bring the book to its natural climax and its ultimate question: *Is this the best that humanity can do?*

I believe the answer is no. I believe we can do better. And I believe that most people *want* to, but just do not see how they can. They view themselves as impotent in the face of the challenges facing our world—challenges created in the main by humanity's own behaviors. There is a way to change those behaviors, but what can the average person do?

Well, plenty, as it turns out. But we'll discuss that in the final pages of this book, titled *In Closing* . . . .

For now, here are the final explosive pages, with their highly unorthodox suggestions on how we might vastly upgrade our collective experience on this planet.

Hang on tight.

16

Since we are discussing larger aspects of life on a planetary scale, as well as reviewing some of the elements of our individual lives which were explored initially in *Book 1*, I would like to ask You about the environment.

What do you want to know?

Is it really being destroyed, as some environmentalists claim, or are these people simply wild-eyed radicals, el-pinko liberal Commies, all of whom graduated from Berkeley and smoke dope?

Yes to both questions.

Whaaa—???

Just kidding. Okay, yes to the first question, no to the second.

The ozone layer *is* depleted? The rain forests *are* being decimated?

Yes. But it is not just about such obvious things. There are matters less obvious about which you should be concerned.

Help me out here.

Well, for instance, there is rapidly developing a soil shortage on your planet. That is, you are running out of good soil in which to grow your food. This is because soil needs time to reconstitute itself, and your corporate farmers *have* no time. They want land that is producing, producing,

producing. So the age-old practice of alternating growing fields from season to season is being abandoned or shortened. To make up for the loss of time, chemicals are being dumped into the land in order to render it fertile faster. Yet in this, as with all things, you cannot develop an artificial substitute for Mother Nature which comes even close to providing what She provides.

The result is that you are eroding, down to a few inches really, in some places, the available nutritive topsoil reserve. In other words, you are growing more and more food in soil which has less and less nutritional content. No irons. No minerals. Nothing which you count on the soil to provide. Worse yet, you are eating foods filled with chemicals which have been poured into the soil in a desperate attempt to reconstitute it. While causing no apparent damage to the body in the short term, you will discover to your sadness that in the long run these trace chemicals, which remain in the body, are not health producing.

This problem of soil erosion through rapid growing-field turnover is not something of which most of your people may be aware, nor is the dwindling growable soil reserve a fantasy made up by yuppie environmentalists looking for their next fashionable cause. Ask any Earth scientist about it and you will hear plenty. It is a problem of epidemic proportions; it is worldwide, and it is serious.

This is just one example of the many ways you are damaging and depleting your Mother, the Earth, the giver of all life, out of a complete disregard for her needs and natural processes.

You are concerned about little on your planet except the satisfying of your own passions, the meeting of your own immediate (and mostly bloated) needs, and quenching the endless human desire for Bigger, Better, More. Yet you might do well as a species to ask, when is enough enough?

Why do we not listen to our environmentalists? Why do we not heed their warnings?

In this, as in all really important matters affecting the quality and style of life on your planet, there is a pattern which is easily discernable. You have coined a phrase in your world which answers the question perfectly. "Follow the money trail."

How can we ever begin to hope to solve these problems when fighting something as massive and insidious as that?

Simple. Eliminate money.

Eliminate money?

Yes. Or at the very least, eliminate its invisibility.

I don't understand.

Most people hide the things they are ashamed of or don't want other people to know about. That is why the largest number of you hide your sexuality, and that is why nearly all of you hide your money. That is to say, you are not open about it. You consider your money to be a very private matter. And therein lies the problem.

If every*one* knew every*thing* about every*body's* money situation, there would be an uprising in your country and on your planet, the likes of which you have never seen. And in the aftermath of that there would be fairness and equity, honesty and true for-the-good-of-all priority in the conduct of human affairs.

It is now not possible to bring fairness or equity, honesty, or the common good to the marketplace because money is so easy to hide. You can actually, physically, take it and *hide it*. There are also all manner of means by which creative accountants can cause corporate money to be "hidden" or to "disappear."

Since money can be hidden, there is no way for anyone to know exactly how much anyone else has or what they are doing with it. This makes it possible for a plethora of inequity, if not to say double-dealing, to exist. Corporations can pay two people vastly different wages for doing the same job, for instance. They can pay one person $57,000 a year while paying the other $42,000 a year, for performing the exactly identical function, giving one employee more than the other simply because the first employee has something the second employee does not.

What's that?

A penis.

Oh.

Yes. Oh, indeed.

But You don't understand. Having a penis makes the first employee more valuable than the second; quicker witted, smarter by half, and, obviously, more capable.

Hmmm. I don't remember constructing you that way. I mean, so unequal in abilities.

Well, You did, and I'm surprised You don't know it. Everyone on this planet knows it.

We'd better stop this now, or people will think we're really serious.

You mean You're not? Well, *we* are! The people on this planet are. That's why women can't be Roman Catholic or Mormon priests, or show up on the wrong side of the Wailing Wall in Jerusalem, or climb to the top job in Fortune 500 companies, or pilot airliners, or—

Yes, we get the point. And *My* point is that pay discrimination, at least, would be much more difficult to get away with if all money transactions were made visible, instead of hidden. Can you imagine what would happen in every workplace on the globe if all companies were forced to publish all the salaries of all the employees? Not the salary *ranges* for particular job classifications, but the *actual compensation awarded* to each individual.

Well, there goes "playing two ends against the middle," right out the window.

Yup.

And there goes, "What he doesn't know won't hurt him."

Yup.

And there goes, "Hey, if we can get her for a third less, why should we pay more?"

Uh-huh.

And there goes apple polishing, and kissing up to the boss, and the "inside track," and company politics, and—

And much, much more would disappear from the workplace, and from the world, through the simple expedient of uncovering the money trail.

Think of it. If you knew exactly how much money each of you holds and the real earnings of all of your industries and corporations and each of their executives—as well as how each person and corporation is *using* the money it has—don't you think that would change things?

Think about this. In what ways do you think things would change?

The plain fact is that people would never put up with 90 percent of what is going on in the world if they *knew* what was going on. Society would never sanction the extraordinarily disproportionate distribution of wealth, much less the means by which it is gained, or the manner in which it is used to gain more, were these facts known, specifically and immediately, by all people everywhere.

Nothing breeds appropriate behavior faster than exposure to the light of public scrutiny. That is why your so-called Sunshine Laws have done so much good in clearing away some of the awful mess of your political and governance system. Public hearings and public accountability has gone far toward eliminating the kinds of backroom antics that went on in the twenties, thirties, forties, and fifties in your town halls and school boards and political precincts—and national government as well.

Now it is time to bring some "sunshine" to the way you deal with compensation for goods and services on your planet.

What are You suggesting?

This is not a suggestion, it is a dare. I dare you to throw out all your money, all your papers and coins and individual national currencies, and start over. Develop an international monetary system that is wide open, totally visible, immediately traceable, completely accountable. Establish a Worldwide Compensation System by which people would be given Credits for services rendered and products produced, and Debits for services used and products consumed.

Everything would be on the system of Credits and Debits. Returns on investments, inheritances, winnings of wagers, salaries and wages, tips and gratuities, everything. And nothing could be purchased without Credits. There would be no other negotiable currency. And everyone's records would be open to everyone else.

It has been said, show me a man's bank account, and I'll show you the man. This system comes close to that scenario. People would, or at least could, know a great deal more about you than they know now. But not only would you know more about each other; you would know more about *everything*. More about what corporations are paying and spending—and what their cost is on an item, as well as their price. (Can you imagine what corporations would do if they had to put *two* figures on every price tag—the price and *their* cost? Would that bring prices down, or what! Would that increase competition, and boost fair trade? You can't even imagine the consequences of such a thing.)

Under the new Worldwide Compensation System, WCS, the transfer of Debits and Credits would be immediate and totally visible. That is, anybody and everybody could inspect the account of any other person or organization at any time. Nothing would be kept secret, nothing would be "private."

The WCS would deduct 10 percent of all earnings each year from the incomes of those *voluntarily requesting* such a deduction. There would be no income tax, no forms to file, no deductions to figure, no "escape hatch" to construct or obfuscation to manufacture! Since all records would be open, everyone in the society would be able to observe who was choosing to offer the 10 percent for the general good of all, and who was not. This voluntary deduction would go toward support of all the programs and services of the government, as voted on by the people.

The whole system would be all very simple, all very visible.

The world would never agree to such a thing.

Of course not. And do you know why? Because such a system would make it impossible for anyone *to do anything they didn't want someone else to know about.* Yet why would you want to do something like that anyway? I'll tell you why. Because currently you live within an interactive social system based on "taking advantage," "getting the edge," "making the most," and "the survival of the so-called fittest."

When the chief aim and goal of your society (as it is in all truly enlightened societies) is the survival of *all;* the benefit, equally, of *all;* the providing of a good life for *all,* then your need for secrecy and quiet dealings and under the table maneuverings and money which can be hidden will disappear.

Do you realize how much good old-fashioned *corruption,* to say nothing of lesser unfairnesses and inequities, would be eliminated through the implementation of such a system?

The secret here, the watchword here, is *visibility.*

Wow. What a concept. What an idea. Absolute visibility in the conduct of our monetary affairs. I keep trying to find a reason why that would be "wrong," why that would not be "okay," but I can't find one.

Of course you can't, *because you've got nothing to hide.* But can you imagine what the people of money and power in the world would do, and how they would scream, if they thought that every move, every purchase, every sale, every dealing, every corporate action and pricing choice and wage negotiation, every decision whatsoever could be reviewed by *anyone* simply looking at the bottom line?

I tell you this: *nothing* breeds fairness faster than *visibility.*

Visibility is simply another word for *truth.*

Know the truth, and the truth shall set you free.

Governments, corporations, people of power know that, which is why they will never allow the truth—the plain and simple truth—to be the basis of any political, social, or economic system they would devise.

In enlightened societies there *are no secrets.* Everyone knows what everyone else has, what everyone else earns, what everyone else pays in wages and taxes and benefits, what every other corporation charges and buys and sells and for how much and for what profit and *everything.* *EVERYTHING.*

Do you know why this is possible only in enlightened societies? Because no one in enlightened societies is willing to get *anything,* or *have* anything, at *someone else's* *expense.*

That is a radical way to live.

It seems radical in primitive societies, yes. In enlightened societies it seems obviously appropriate.

I am intrigued by this concept of "visibility." Could it extend beyond monetary affairs? Might it be a watchword for our personal relationships as well?

One would hope so.

And yet it isn't.

As a rule, no. Not yet on your planet. Most people still have too much to hide.

Why? What's that about?

In personal relationships (and in all relationships, really) it's about *loss.* It's about being afraid of what one might lose or fail to gain. Yet the best personal relationships, and certainly the best romantic ones, are relationships in which everyone knows everything; in which *visibility* is not only the watchword, but the *only word;* in which there simply are no secrets. In these relationships nothing is withheld, nothing is shaded or colored or hidden or disguised. Nothing is left out or unspoken. There is no guesswork, there is no game playing; no one is "doing a dance," "running a number," or "shining you on."

But if everyone knew everything we were thinking—

229

Hold it. This isn't about having no mental privacy, no safe space in which to move through your personal process. That's not what I'm talking about here.

This is about simply being open and honest in your dealings with another. This is about simply telling the truth when you speak, and about withholding no truth when you know it should be spoken. This is about never again lying, or shading, or verbally or mentally manipulating, or twisting your truth into the hundred and one other contortions which typify the largest number of human communications.

This is about coming clean, telling it like it is, giving it to them straight. This is about ensuring that all individuals have all the data and know everything they need to know on a subject. This is about fairness and openness and, well . . . *visibility*.

Yet this does not mean that every single thought, every private fear, every darkest memory, every fleeting judgment, opinion, or reaction must be placed on the table for discussion and examination. That is not visibility, that is insanity, and it will make you crazy.

We are talking here about simple, direct, straightforward, open, honest, complete communication. Yet even at that, it is a striking concept, and a little-used one.

You can say that again.

Yet even at that, it is a striking concept, and a little-used one.

You should have been in vaudeville.

Are you kidding? I am.

But seriously, this is a magnificent idea. Imagine, an entire society built around the Principle of Visibility. Are You sure it would work?

I'll tell you something. Half the world's ills would go away tomorrow. Half the world's worries, half the world's conflicts, half the world's anger, half the world's frustration . . .

Oh, there would be anger and frustration at first, make no mistake about that. When it was finally discovered just how much the average person *is* being played like a fiddle, used like a disposable commodity, manipulated, lied to, and downright cheated, there would be *plenty* of frustration and anger. But "visibility" would clean most of that up within 60 days; make it go away.

Let me invite you again—just think about it.

Do you think you could live a life like this? No more secrets? Absolute visibility?

If not, why not?

What are you keeping from others that you don't want them to know?

What are you saying to someone that isn't true?

What are you not saying to someone that is?

Has lying by omission or commission brought your world where you really want it to be? Has manipulation (of the marketplace, of a particular situation, or simply of a person) through silence and secrecy really benefited us? Is "privacy" really what makes our governmental, corporate, and individual lives work?

What would happen if everybody could see everything?

Now there is an irony here. Don't you see that this is the one thing you fear about your first meeting with God? Don't you get that what you've been afraid of is that the gig is up, the game is over, the tap dance is finished, the shadow boxing is done, and the long, long trail of deceits, big and small, has come to—quite literally—a *dead end*?

Yet the good news is that there is no reason for fear, no cause to be scared. No one is going to judge you, no one is going to make you "wrong," no one is going to throw you into the everlasting fires of hell.

(And to you Roman Catholics, no, you won't even go to purgatory.)

(And to you Mormons, no, you won't be trapped forever in the lowest heaven, unable to get to "highest heaven," nor will you be labeled Sons of Perdition and banished forever to realms unknown.)

(And to you . . .)

Well, you get the picture. Each of you has constructed, within the framework of your own particular theology, some idea, some concept of God's Worst Punishment. And I hate to tell you this, because I see the fun you're having with the drama of it all, but, well . . . *just ain't no such thing.*

Perhaps when you lose the fear of having your life become totally visible at the moment of your death, you can get over the fear of having your life become totally visible *while you are living it.*

Wouldn't *that* be something. . . .

Yes, wouldn't it, though? So here's the formula to help you get started. Turn back to the very beginning of this book and review again the *Five Levels of Truth Telling.* Determine to memorize this model and implement it. Seek the truth, say the truth, live the truth every day. Do this with yourself and with every person whose life you touch.

Then get ready to be naked. Stand by for *visibility.*

This feels scary. This feels real scary.

Look to see what you are afraid of.

I'm afraid everyone will leave the room. I'm afraid no one will like me any more.

I see. You feel you have to lie to get people to like you?

Not lie, exactly. Just not tell them *everything*.

Remember what I said before. This is not about blurting out every little feeling, thought, idea, fear, memory, confession, or whatever. This is simply about always speaking the truth, showing yourself completely. With your dearest loved one you can be physically naked, can you not?

Yes.

Then why not be emotionally naked as well?

The second is much harder than the first.

I understand that. That does not fail to recommend it, however, for the rewards are great.

Well, You've certainly brought up some interesting ideas. Abolish hidden agendas, build a society on visibility, tell the truth all the time to everyone about everything. Whew!

On these few concepts entire societies have been constructed. Enlightened societies.

I haven't found any.

I wasn't speaking of your planet.

Oh.

Or even your solar system.

OH.

But you don't have to leave the planet or even leave your house to begin experiencing what such a New Thought system would be like. Start in your own family, in your own home. If you own a business, start in your own company. Tell everyone in your firm exactly what you make, what the company is making and spending, and what each and every employee makes. You will shock the hell out of them. I mean that quite literally. You will shock the hell *right out of them*. If everyone who owned a company did this, work would no longer be a living hell for so many because a greater sense of equity, fair play, and appropriate compensation would automatically come to the workplace.

Tell your customers exactly what a product or service costs you to provide. Put those two numbers on your price tag: your cost and your price. Can you still be proud of what you are asking? Do you encounter any fear that someone will think you are "ripping them off" should they know your cost/price ratio? If so, look to see what kind of adjustment you want to make in your pricing to bring it back down into the realm of basic fairness, rather than "get what you can while the gettin's good."

I dare you to do this. I dare you.

It will require a complete change in your thinking. You will have to be just as concerned with your customers or clients as you are with yourself.

Yes, you can begin to build this New Society right now, right here, today. The choice is yours. You can continue to support the old system, the present paradigm, or you can blaze the trail and show your world a new way.

You can *be* that new way. In everything. Not just in business, not just in your personal relationships, not just in politics or economics or religion or this aspect or that of the overall life experience, but in *everything*.

Be the new way. Be the higher way. Be the grandest way. Then you can truly say, *I am the way and the life. Follow me.*

If the whole world followed you, would you be pleased with where you took it?

Let that be your question for the day.

17

I hear Your challenge. I hear it. Please tell me more now about life on this planet on a grander scale. Tell me how nation can get along with nation so there will be "war no more."

There will always be disagreements between nations, for disagreement is merely a sign—and a healthy one—of individuality. *Violent resolution* of disagreements, however, is a sign of extraordinary immaturity.

There is no reason in the world why violent resolution cannot be avoided, given the willingness of nations to avoid it.

One would think that the massive toll in death and destroyed lives would be enough to produce such willingness, but among primitive cultures such as yours, that is not so.

As long as you think you can win an argument, you will have it. As long as you think you can win a war, you will fight it.

What is the answer to all of this?

I do not have an answer, I only have—

I know, I know! An observation.

Yes. I observe now what I observed before. A short-term answer could be to establish what some have called a one-world government, with a world court to settle disputes (one whose verdicts may not be ignored, as happens with the present World Court) and a world peacekeeping force to guarantee that no one nation—no matter how powerful or how influential—can ever again aggress upon another.

Yet understand that there may still be violence upon the Earth. The peacekeeping force may *have* to use violence to get someone to *stop* doing so. As I noted in *Book 1*, failure to stop a despot empowers a despot. Sometimes the only way to *avoid* a war is to *have* a war. Sometimes you have to do what you don't *want* to do in order to ensure that you won't *have to keep on doing it!* This apparent contradiction is part of the Divine Dichotomy, which says that sometimes the only way to ultimately *Be* a thing—in this case, "peaceful"—may be, at first, to *not* be it!

In other words, often the only way to know yourself as That Which You Are is to experience yourself as That Which You Are *Not*.

It is an observable truth that power in your world can no longer rest disproportionately with any individual nation, but must rest in the hands of the total group of nations existing on this planet. Only in this way can the world finally be at peace, resting in the secure knowledge that no despot—no matter how big or powerful his individual nation—can or will ever again infringe upon the territories of another nation, nor threaten her freedoms.

No longer need the smallest nations depend upon the goodwill of the largest nations, often having to bargain away their own resources and offer their prime lands for foreign military bases in order to earn it. Under this new system, the security of the smallest nations will be guaranteed not by whose back they scratch, but by who is backing *them*.

All 160 nations would rise up should one nation be invaded. All 160 nations would say *No!* should one nation be violated or threatened in any way.

Similarly, nations would no longer be threatened economically, blackmailed into certain courses of action by their bigger trading partners, required to meet certain "guidelines" in order to receive foreign aid, or mandated to perform in certain ways in order to qualify for simple humanitarian assistance.

Yet there are those among you who would argue that such a system of global governance would erode the independence and the greatness of individual nations. The truth is, it would *increase* it—and that is precisely what the largest nations, whose independence is assured by power, not by law or justice, are afraid of. For then no longer would only the largest nation always get its way automatically, but the considerations of all nations would have to be heard equally. And no longer would the largest nations be able to control and hoard the mass of the world's resources, but would be required to share them more equally, render them accessible more readily, provide their benefits more uniformly to *all* the world's people.

A worldwide government would level the playing field—and this idea, while driving to the core of the debate regarding basic human dignity, is anathema to the world's "haves," who want the "have-nots" to go seek their *own* fortunes—ignoring, of course, the fact that the "haves" *control* all that others would seek.

Yet it feels as though we are talking about redistribution of wealth here. How can we maintain the incentive of those who *do* want more, and are willing to work for it, if they know they must share with those who do not care to work that hard?

First, it is not merely a question of those who *want* to "work hard" and those who don't. That is a simplistic way to cast the argument (usually constructed in that way by the "haves"). It is more often a question of opportunity than willingness. So the real job, and the first job in restructuring the social order, is to make sure each person and each nation has equal *opportunity*.

> That can never happen so long as those who currently possess and control the mass of the world's wealth and resources hold tightly to that control.

Yes. I mentioned Mexico, and without wanting to get into "nation bashing," I think this country provides an excellent example of that. A handful of rich and powerful families control the wealth and resources of that entire nation—and have for 40 years. "Elections" in this so-called Western Democracy are a farce because the same families have controlled the same political party for decades, assuring virtually no serious opposition. Result? "The rich get richer and the poor get poorer."

If wages should jump from $1.75 to a whopping $3.15 an hour, the rich point to how much they've done for the poor in providing jobs and opportunity for economic advancement. Yet the only ones making quantum advances are the *rich*—the industrialists and business owners who sell their commodities on the national and world market at huge profits, given the low cost of their labor.

America's rich know this is true—which is why many of America's rich and powerful are rebuilding their plants and factories in Mexico and other foreign countries where slave-labor wages are considered a grand opportunity for the peasants. Meanwhile, these workers toil in unhealthy and wholly unsafe conditions, but the local government—controlled by the same few reaping the profits from these ventures—imposes few regulations. Health and safety standards and environmental protections are virtually nonexistent in the workplace.

The people are not being cared for, nor is the Earth, on which they are being asked to live in their paper shacks next to streams in which they do their laundry and into which they sometimes defecate—for indoor plumbing is also often not one of their dignities.

What is created by such crass disregard for the masses is a population which cannot afford the very products it is manufacturing. But the rich factory owners don't care. They can ship their goods to other nations where there are people who can.

Yet I believe that sooner or later this spiral will turn in upon itself—with devastating consequences. Not just in Mexico, but wherever humans are exploited.

Revolutions and civil war are inevitable, as are wars between nations, so long as the "haves" continue seeking to exploit the "have-nots" under the guise of providing *opportunity*.

Holding on to the wealth and the resources has become so *institutionalized* that it almost now appears *acceptable* even to some fair-minded people, who see it as simply open market economics.

Yet only the *power* held by the world's wealthy individuals and nations makes that illusion of fairness possible. The truth is, it is *not* fair to the largest percentage of the world's people and nations, who are held down from even attempting to achieve what the Powerful have achieved.

The system of governance described here would drastically shift the balance of power away from the resource-rich to the resource-poor, forcing the resources themselves to be fairly shared.

This is what the powerful fear.

Yes. So the short-term solution to the world's foment may be a new social structure—a new, worldwide, government.

There have been those leaders among you who have been insightful enough and brave enough to propose the beginnings of such a new world order. Your George Bush, whom history will judge to be a man of far greater wisdom, vision, compassion, and courage than contemporary society was willing or able to acknowledge, was such a leader. So was Soviet President Mikhail Gorbachev, the first communist head of state ever to win the Nobel Peace

Prize and a man who proposed enormous political changes, virtually ending what you've called the Cold War. And so was your President Carter, who brought your Mr. Begin and Mr. Sadat to come to agreements no one else ever had dreamt of, and who, long after his presidency, pulled the world back from violent confrontation time and time again through the simple assertion of a simple truth: No one's point of view is less worthy of being heard than another's; No one human being has less dignity than another.

It is interesting that these courageous leaders, each of whom brought the world from the brink of war in their own time, and each of whom espoused and proposed massive movements away from the prevailing political structure, each served only one term, removed from office as they were by the very people they were seeking to elevate. Incredibly popular worldwide, they were soundly rejected at home. It is said that a man is without honor in his own home. In the case of these men, it is because their vision was miles ahead of their people, who could see only limited, parochial concerns, and imagined nothing but loss proceeding from these larger visions.

So, too, has every leader who has dared to step out and call for the end of oppression by the powerful been discouraged and defiled.

Thus it will always be until a *long*-term solution, *which is not a political one*, is put into place. That long-term solution—and the only real one—is a New Awareness, and a New Consciousness. An awareness of Oneness and a consciousness of Love.

The incentive to succeed, to make the most of one's life, should not be economic or materialistic reward. It is misplaced there. This misplaced priority is what has created all of the problems we have discussed here.

When the incentive for greatness is not economic—when economic security and basic materialistic needs are guaranteed to all—then incentive will not disappear, but be of a different sort, *increasing* in strength and determination, producing *true* greatness, not the kind of transparent, transient "greatness" which present incentives produce.

But why isn't living a better life, creating a better life for our children, a good incentive?

"Living a better life" *is* a proper incentive. Creating a "better life" for your children *is* a good incentive. But the question is, what makes for a "better life"?

How do you define "better"? How do you define "life"?

If you define "better" as *bigger, better, more* money, power, sex, and *stuff* (houses, cars, clothes, CD collections—whatever) . . . and if you define "life" as the period elapsing between birth and death in this your present existence, then you're doing nothing to get out of the trap that has *created* your planet's predicament.

Yet if you define "better" as a larger experience and a greater expression of your grandest State of Being, and "life" as an eternal, ongoing, never-ending process of *Being*, you may yet find your way.

A "better life" is not created by the accumulation of things. Most of you know this, all of you say you understand it, yet your lives—and the decisions you make which drive your lives—have as much to do with "things" as anything else, and usually more.

You strive for things, you work for things, and when you get some of the things you want, you never let them go.

The incentive of most of humankind is to achieve, acquire, obtain *things*. Those who do not care about things let them go easily.

Because your present incentive for greatness has to do with accumulation of all the world has to offer, all of the world is in various stages of struggle. Enormous *portions* of the population are still struggling for simple physical survival.

Each day is filled with anxious moments, desperate measures. The mind is concerned with basic, vital questions. Will there be enough food? Is shelter available? Will we be warm? *Enormous* numbers of people are still concerned with these matters daily. Thousands *die* each month for lack of food alone.

Smaller numbers of people are able to reasonably rely on the basics of survival appearing in their lives, but struggle to provide something more—a modicum of security, a modest but decent home, a better tomorrow. They work hard, they fret about how and whether they'll ever "get ahead." The mind is concerned with urgent, worrisome questions.

By far the smallest number of people have all they could ever ask for—indeed, everything the other two groups *are* asking for—but, interestingly, many in this last group are still *asking for more.*

Their minds are concerned with *holding on to* all that they have acquired and increasing their holdings.

Now, in addition to these three groups, there is a fourth. It is the smallest group of all. In fact, it is tiny.

This group has detached itself from the need for material things. It is concerned with spiritual truth, spiritual reality, and spiritual experience.

The people in this group see life as a spiritual encounter—a journey of the soul. They respond to all human events within that context. They hold all human experience within that paradigm. Their struggle has to do with the search for God, the fulfillment of Self, the expression of truth.

As they evolve, this struggle becomes not a struggle at all, but a process. It is a process of Self-definition (not self-discovery), of Growth (not learning), of Being (not doing).

The *reason* for seeking, striving, searching, stretching, and *succeeding* becomes completely different. The reason for doing *anything* is changed, and with it the doer is likewise changed. The reason becomes the process, and the doer becomes a be-er.

Whereas, before, the reason for reaching, for striving, for working hard all of one's life was to provide worldly things, now the reason is to experience heavenly things.

Whereas, before, the concerns were largely the concerns of the body, now the concerns are largely the concerns of the soul.

Everything has moved, everything has shifted. The purpose of life has changed, and so has life itself.

The "incentive for greatness" has shifted, and with it the need for coveting, acquiring, protecting, and increasing worldly possessions has disappeared.

Greatness will no longer be measured by how much one has accumulated. The world's resources will rightly be seen as belonging to all the world's people. In a world blessed with sufficient abundance to meet the basic needs of all, the basic needs of all *will be met.*

Everyone will *want* it that way. There will no longer be a need to subject anyone to an involuntary tax. You will all *volunteer* to send 10 percent of your harvest and your abundance to programs supporting those whose harvest is less. It will no longer be possible for thousands to stand by watching thousands of others starve—not for lack of food, but for lack of sufficient human *will* to create a simple political mechanism by which people can *get* the food.

Such moral obscenities—now commonplace among your primitive society—will be erased forever the day you change your incentive for greatness and your definition of it.

Your new incentive: to become what I created you to be—the physical out-picturing of Deity Itself.

When you choose to be Who You Really Are—God made manifest—you will never again act in an ungodly manner. No longer will you have to display bumper stickers which read:

GOD SAVE ME
FROM YOUR FOLLOWERS

18

Let me see if I'm tracking this. What seems to be emerging here is a world view of equality and equanimity, where all nations submit to one world government, and all people share in the world's riches.

> Remember when you talk about equality that we're meaning equal *opportunity,* not equality *in fact.*
>
> Actual "equality" will never be achieved, and be grateful that is so.

Why?

> Because equality is sameness—and the last thing the world needs is sameness.
>
> No—I am not arguing here for a world of automatons, each receiving identical allotments from a Big Brother Central Government.
>
> I am speaking of a world in which two things are guaranteed:
>
> 1. The meeting of basic needs.
> 2. The opportunity to go higher.
>
> With all your world's resources, with all your abundance, you have not yet managed those two simple things. Instead, you have trapped millions on the lowest end of the socioeconomic scale and devised a world view that systematically keeps them there. You are allowing thousands to die each year for lack of simple basics.
>
> For all the world's magnificence, you have not found a way to be magnificent enough to stop people from starving to death, much less stop killing each other. You

actually let *children* starve to death right in front of you. You actually kill people because they disagree with you.

You are primitive.

And we think we are so advanced.

The first mark of a primitive society is that it thinks itself advanced. The first mark of a primitive consciousness is that it thinks itself enlightened.

So let's summarize it. The way we'll get to the first step on the ladder, where these two fundamental guarantees are accorded everyone. . . .

Is through two shifts, two changes—one in your political paradigm, one in your spiritual.

The movement to a unified world government would include a greatly empowered world court to resolve international disputes and a peacekeeping force to give power to the laws by which you choose to govern yourselves.

The world government would include a Congress of Nations—two representatives from every nation on Earth—and a People's Assembly—with representation in direct proportion to a nation's population.

Exactly the way the U.S. Government is set up—with two houses, one providing proportional representation and one providing equal voice to all of the states.

Yes. Your U.S. Constitution was God inspired.

The same balance of powers should be built in to the new world constitution.

There would be, likewise, an executive branch, legislative branch, and a judicial branch.

Each nation would keep its internal peacekeeping police, but all national armies would be disbanded— exactly as each of your individual states disbanded their armies and navies in favor of a federal peacekeeping force serving the entire group of states you now call a nation.

Nations would reserve the right to form and call up their own militia on a moment's notice, just as your states each have the constitutional right to keep and activate a state militia.

And—just as your states do now—each of the 160 Nation States in the union of nations would have the right to secede from the union based upon a vote of the people (though why it would want to do so is beyond Me, given that its people would be more secure and more abundant than ever before).

And—once more for those of us who are slow—such a unified world federation would produce—?

1. An end to wars between nations and the settling of disputes by killing.

2. An end to abject poverty, death by starvation, and mass exploitation of people and resources by those of power.

3. An end to the systematic environmental destruction of the Earth.

4. An escape from the endless struggle for bigger, better, more.

5. An opportunity—*truly* equal—for *all* people to rise to the highest expression of Self.

6. An end to all limitations and discriminations holding people back—whether in housing, in the workplace, or in the political system, or in personal sexual relationships.

Would your new world order require a redistribution of wealth?

It would require nothing. It would *produce*, voluntarily and quite automatically, a redistribution of *resources*.

All people would be offered a proper education, for instance. *All* people would be offered open opportunity to use that education in the workplace—to follow careers which bring them *joy*.

All people would be guaranteed access to health care whenever and however needed.

All people would be guaranteed they won't starve to death or have to live without sufficient clothing or adequate shelter.

All people would be granted the basic dignities of life so that *survival* would never again be the issue, so that simple comforts and basic dignities were provided *all* human beings.

Even if they did nothing to earn it?

Your thought that these things need to be *earned* is the basis for your thought that you have to *earn your way to heaven*. Yet you cannot earn your way into God's good graces, and you do not have to, because you are already there. This is something you cannot accept, because it is something you cannot *give*. When you learn to *give* unconditionally (which is to say, *love* unconditionally), then will you learn to *receive* unconditionally.

This life was created as a vehicle through which you might be allowed to experience that.

Try to wrap yourself around this thought: People have a right to basic survival. Even if they do *nothing*. Even if they contribute *nothing*. Survival with dignity is one of the basic rights of life. I have given you enough resources to be able to guarantee that to everyone. All you have to do is share.

But then what would stop people from simply wasting their lives, lollygagging around, collecting "benefits"?

First of all, it is not yours to judge what is a life wasted. Is a life wasted if a person does nothing but lie around thinking of poetry for 70 years, then comes up with a single sonnet which opens a door of understanding and insight for thousands of people? Is a life wasted if a person lies, cheats, schemes, damages, manipulates, and hurts others all his life, but then remembers something of his true nature as a result of it—remembers, perhaps, something he has been spending lifetimes trying to remember—and thus evolves, at last, to the Next Level? Is that life "wasted"?

It is not for you to judge the journey of another's soul. It is for you to decide who YOU are, not who another has been or has failed to be.

So, you ask what would stop people from simply wasting their lives, lollygagging around, collecting "benefits," and the answer is: nothing.

But do You really think this would work? You don't think those who *are* contributing wouldn't begin to resent those who are not?

Yes, they would, if they are not enlightened. Yet enlightened ones would look upon the noncontributors with great compassion, not resentment.

Compassion?

Yes, because the contributors would realize that noncontributors are missing the greatest opportunity and the grandest glory: the opportunity to create and the glory of experiencing the *highest idea* of Who They Really Are. And the contributors would know that this was punishment enough for their laziness, if, indeed, punishment were required—which it is not.

But wouldn't those who are really contributing be angry at having the fruits of their labor taken from them and given to the lazy ones?

You are not listening. *All* would be given minimal survival portions. Those who have more would be given an opportunity to contribute 10 percent of their earnings in order to make this possible.

As to how income would be decided, the open marketplace would determine the value of one's contribution, just as it does today in your country.

But then we would *still* have the "rich" and the "poor," just as we do today! That is not *equality*.

But it is equal *opportunity*. For everyone would have the *opportunity* to live a basic existence without worries of survival. And everyone would be given an equal opportunity to acquire knowledge, develop skills, and use his or her natural talents in the Joy Place.

The Joy Place?

That's what the "work place" will then be called.

But won't there still be envy?

Envy, yes. Jealousy, no. Envy is a natural emotion urging you to strive to be more. It is the two-year-old child yearning and urging herself to reach that doorknob which her big brother can reach. There is nothing wrong with that. There is nothing wrong with envy. It is a motivator. It is pure desire. It gives birth to greatness.

Jealousy, on the other hand, is a fear-driven emotion making one willing for the other to have less. It is an emotion often based in bitterness. It proceeds from anger and leads to anger. And it kills. Jealousy can kill. Anyone who's been in a jealous triangle knows that.

Jealousy kills, envy gives birth.

Those who are envious will be given every opportunity to succeed in *their* own way. No one will be held back economically, politically, socially. Not by reason of race, gender or sexual orientation. Not by reason of birth, class status or age. Nor for any reason at all. Discrimination for *any* reason will simply no longer be tolerated.

And yes, there may still be the "rich" and the "poor," but there will no longer be the "starving" and the "desti-tute."

You see, the incentive *won't* be taken out of life . . . *merely the desperation.*

But what will guarantee that we'll have enough contributors to "carry" the noncontributors?

The greatness of the human spirit.

Oh?

Contrary to your apparent dire belief, the average per-son will *not* be satisfied with subsistence levels and noth-ing more. In addition, the whole incentive for greatness will change when the second paradigm shift—the spiritual shift—takes place.

What would cause such a shift? It hasn't occurred yet in the 2,000-year history—

Try two-*billion*-year history—

—of the planet. Why should it occur now?

Because with the shift away from material survival—with the elimination of the need to succeed mightily in order to acquire a modicum of security—there will be no other reason to achieve, to stand out, to become magnif-icent, save *the experience of magnificence itself!*

And that will be sufficient motivation?

The human spirit rises; it does not fall in the face of true opportunity. The soul seeks a higher experience of itself, not a lower. Anyone who has experienced *true magnificence*, if only for a moment, knows this.

How about power? In this special reordering, there would still be those with inordinate wealth and power.

Financial earnings would be limited.

Oh, boy—here we go. You want to explain how that would work before I explain why it won't?

Yes. Just as there would be lower limits on income, so would there be upper limits. First, nearly everyone will tithe 10 percent of their income to the world government. This is the voluntary 10 percent deduction I mentioned before.

Yes . . . the old "equal tax" proposal.

In your present society at this present time it would have to take the form of a tax because you are not sufficiently enlightened to see that voluntary deduction for the general good of all is in your best interest. Yet when the shift in consciousness I have been describing occurs, such an open, caring, freely offered deduction from your harvest will be seen by you as obviously appropriate.

I have to tell You something. Do You mind if I interrupt You here to tell You something?

No, go right ahead.

This conversation is seeming very strange to me. I never thought I'd have a conversation with God in which God would start recommending political courses of action. I mean, really. How do I convince people that *God is for the flat tax!*

Well, I see you keep insisting on seeing it as a "tax," but I understand that, because the concept of simply offering to share 10 percent of your abundance seems so foreign to you. Nevertheless, why do you find it difficult to believe I would have an idea about this?

I thought God was nonjudgmental, had no opinion, didn't care about such things.

Wait, let me get this straight. In our last conversation—which you called *Book 1*—I answered all sorts of questions. Questions about what makes relationships work, questions about right livelihood, questions about diet, even. How does that differ from this?

I don't know. It just *seems* different. I mean, do You really have a political point of view? Are You a card-carrying Republican? What a truth to come out of this book! God is a *Republican*.

You'd rather I be a Democrat? Good God!

Cute. No, I'd rather you be *apolitical*.

I am apolitical. I have no political point of view whatsoever.

Sort of like Bill Clinton.

Hey, good! Now *you're* being cute! I like humor, don't you?

I guess I didn't expect God to be humorous *or* political.

Or anything human, eh?

Okay, let Me place this book and *Book 1*, for that matter, into context for you once again.

I have no preference in the matter of how you conduct your life. My only desire is that you experience yourself fully as a creative being, so that you might know Who You Really Are.

Good. I understand that. So far, so good.

Every question I have answered here and every inquiry to which I responded in *Book 1* has been heard and responded to within the context of what you, as a creative being, say you are attempting to be and do. For instance, in *Book 1* you asked Me many questions about how you could finally make relationships work. Do you remember?

Yes, of course.

Did you find My answers so problematic? Did you find it difficult to believe that I would have a point of view on this?

I never thought about it. I just read the answers.

Yet, you see, I was placing My answers within the context of your questions. That is, given that you desire to be or do so-and-so, what is a way to go about that? And I showed you a way.

Yes, You did.

I am doing the same thing here.

It's just . . . I don't know . . . more difficult to believe that God would say these things than it was to believe that God would say those things.

Are you finding it more difficult to *agree with* some of the things said here?

Well . . .

Because if you are, that's very okay.

It is?

Of course.

It's okay to disagree with God?

Certainly. What do you think I'm going to do, squash you like an insect?

I hadn't gotten that far in my thinking, actually.

Look, the world has been disagreeing with Me since this whole thing started. Hardly anyone has been doing it My Way since it began.

That's true, I guess.

You can be sure it's true. Had people been following My instructions—left with you through hundreds of teachers over thousands of years—the world would be a much different place. So if you wish to disagree with Me now, go right ahead. Besides, I could be wrong.

What?

I said, besides, I could be wrong. Oh, my goodness . . . you're not taking this all as *gospel,* are you?

You mean I'm not supposed to put any stock in this dialogue?

Oops, hold it. I think you've missed a big part of all this. Let's go back to Square One: *You're making this all up.*

Oh, well, that's a relief. For a while there I thought I was actually getting some real guidance.

The guidance you are getting is to *follow your heart.* Listen to your *soul.* Hear your *self.* Even when I present you with an option, an idea, a point of view, you are under no obligation to accept that as your own. If you disagree, then *disagree*. That is *the whole point of this exercise*. The idea wasn't for you to substitute your dependency on everything and everyone else *with a dependency on this book*. The idea was to cause you to *think*. To think for your *self*. And that is who I Am right now. I am you, *thinking*. I am you, thinking out loud.

You mean this material is not coming from the Highest Source?

Of course it is! Yet here is the one thing you still cannot believe: *you are the Highest Source*. And here is the one thing you still apparently do not grasp: *you are creating it all—all of your life—right here, right now*. You . . . YOU . . . are creating it. Not Me. YOU.

So . . . are there some answers to these purely political questions that you do not like? *Then change them*. Do it. Now. Before you start hearing them as *gospel*. Before you start making them *real*. Before you start calling your last thought about something more important, more valid, more true than your *next* thought.

Remember, it's always your *new thought* that creates your reality. Always.

Now, do you find anything in this political discussion of ours that you want to change?

Well, not really. I'm sort of agreeing with You, as it happens. I just didn't know what to make of all of this.

Make of it what you wish. Don't you get it? *That's what you're doing with all of life!*

Okay, all right . . . I think I've got it. I would like to continue with this conversation, if only to see where it's going.

Fine, then let's do that.

You were about to say . . .

I was about to say that in other societies—enlightened societies—the putting aside of a set amount of what one receives (what you call "income") to be used for the general good of the society itself is a rather common practice. Under the new system we have been exploring for your society, everyone would earn as much each year as they could—and they would retain what they earn, up to a certain limit.

What limit?

An arbitrary limit, agreed to by everyone.

And anything above that limit?

Would be contributed to the world charitable trust *in the name of the contributor*, so all the world would know its benefactors.

Benefactors would have the option of direct control over the disbursement of 60 percent of their contribution, providing them the satisfaction of putting most of their money exactly where they want it.

The other 40 percent would be allocated to programs legislated by the world federation and administered by it.

If people knew that after a certain income limit everything would be taken from them, what would be their incentive to keep working? What would cause them not to stop in midstream, once they reached their income "limit"?

Some would. So what? Let them stop. Mandatory work above the income limit, with contributions to the world charitable trust, would not be required. The money saved from the elimination of mass production of weapons of war would be sufficient to supply everyone's basic need. The 10 percent tithe of all that is earned worldwide on top of those savings would elevate all of society, not just the chosen few, to a new level of dignity and abundance. And the contribution of earnings above the agreed-upon limit would produce such widespread opportunity and satisfaction for everyone that jealousy and social angers would virtually disintegrate.

So some *would* stop working—especially those who *saw* their life activity as *real work.* Yet those who saw their activity as *absolute joy* would *never* stop.

Not everyone can have a job like that.

Untrue. Everyone can.

Joy at the work place has nothing to do with function, and everything to do with purpose.

The mother who wakes up at 4 o'clock in the morning to change her baby's diaper understands this perfectly. She hums and coos to the baby, and for all the world it doesn't look like what she is doing is any work at all. Yet it is her attitude about what she is doing, it is her intention with regard to it, it is her *purpose* in undertaking this activity, which make the activity a true joy.

I have used this example of motherhood before, because the love of a mother for her child is as close as you may be able to come to understanding some of the concepts of which I am speaking in this book and in this trilogy.

Still, what would be the purpose of eliminating "limitless earning potential"? Wouldn't that rob the human experience of one of its greatest opportunities, one of its most glorious adventures?

You would still have the opportunity and the adventure of earning a ridiculous amount of money. The upper limit on retainable income would be very high—more than the average person . . . the average ten people . . . would ever need. And the amount of income you could *earn* would not be limited—simply the amount you would choose to retain for personal use. The remainder—everything, say, over $25 million a year (I use a strictly arbitrary figure to make a point)—would be spent for programs and services benefitting all humankind.

As to the reason—the *why* of it . . .

The upper retainable income limit would be a reflection of a consciousness shift on the planet; an awareness that the highest purpose of life is not the accumulation of the greatest wealth, but the doing of the greatest good—and a corollary awareness that, indeed, the *concentration of wealth*, not the sharing of it, is the largest single factor in the creation of the world's most persistent and striking social and political dilemmas.

The opportunity to amass wealth—unlimited wealth—is the cornerstone of the capitalistic system, a system of free enterprise and open competition that has produced the greatest society the world has ever known.

The problem is, you really believe that.

No, I don't. But I've mouthed it here on behalf of those who *do* believe it.

Those who do believe it are terribly deluded and see nothing of the current reality on your planet.

In the United States, the top one and a half percent hold more wealth than the bottom 90 percent. The net worth of the richest 834,000 people is nearly a trillion dollars greater than the poorest *84 million people combined.*

So? They've worked for it.

You Americans tend to see class status as a function of individual effort. Some have "made good," so you assume that anybody can. That view is simplistic and naive. It assumes that everyone has equal opportunity, when in fact, in America just as in Mexico, the rich and powerful strive and contrive to hold on to their money and their power *and to increase it*.

So? What's wrong with that?

They *do* so by systematically *eliminating* competition, by institutionally *minimizing* true opportunity, and by collectively *controlling* the flow and the growth of wealth.

This they accomplish through all manner of devices, from unfair labor practices which exploit the masses of the world's poor to good-old-boy network competitive practices which minimize (and all but destroy) a newcomer's chances of entering the Inner Circle of the successful.

They then seek to control public policy and governmental programs around the world to *further* ensure that the masses of people remain regulated, controlled, and subservient.

I don't believe that the rich do this. Not the largest number of them. There may be a handful of conspirators, I suppose. . . .

In most cases it isn't rich *individuals* who do it; it's the social systems and institutions they represent. Those systems and institutions were *created* by the rich and powerful—and it is the rich and powerful who continue to support them.

By standing behind such social systems and institutions, individuals can wash their hands of any personal responsibility for the conditions which oppress the masses while favoring the rich and powerful.

For example, let's go back to health care in America. Millions of America's poor have no access to preventive medical care. One cannot point to any *individual doctor* and say, "this is your doing, it is your fault" that, in the richest nation on Earth, millions cannot get in to see a doctor unless they're in dire straits in an emergency room.

No *individual* doctor is to blame for that, yet *all doctors benefit.* The entire medical profession—and every allied industry—enjoys unprecedented profits from a delivery system which has *institutionalized* discrimination against the working poor and the unemployed.

And that's just one example of how the "system" keeps the rich rich and the poor poor.

The point is that it is the rich and powerful who support such social structures and *staunchly resist any real effort to change them.* They stand against any political or economic approach which seeks to provide true opportunity and genuine dignity to all people.

Most of the rich and powerful, taken individually, are certainly nice enough people, with as much compassion and sympathy as anyone. But mention a concept as threatening to *them* as yearly income limits (even ridiculously high limits, such as $25 million annually), and they start whining about usurpation of individual rights, erosion of the "American way," and "lost incentives."

Yet what about the right of *all* people to live in minimally decent surroundings, with enough food to keep from starving, enough clothing to stay warm? What about the right of people *everywhere* to have adequate health care—the right not to have to *suffer* or *die* from relatively minor medical complications which those with money overcome with the snap of a finger?

The resources of your planet—*including* the *fruits of the labors* of the masses of the indescribably poor who are continually and systematically exploited—belong to all the world's people, not just those who are rich and powerful enough to do the exploiting.

And here is how the exploitation works: Your rich industrialists go into a country or an area where there is no work at all, where the people are destitute, where there is abject poverty. The rich set up a factory there, offering those poor people jobs—sometimes 10-, 12-, and 14-hour-a-day jobs—at substandard, if not to say *sub-human,* wages. Not enough, mind you, to allow those workers to escape their rat-infested villages, but just enough to let them live *that* way, as opposed to having *no food or shelter at all.*

And when they are called on it, these capitalists say, *"Hey,* they've got it better than *before,* don't they? We've *improved their lot!* The people are *taking* the jobs, aren't they? Why, we've brought them *opportunity!* And *we're* taking all the *risk!"*

Yet how much risk is there in paying people 75 cents an hour to manufacture sneakers which are going to sell for $125 a pair?

Is this risk-taking or exploitation, pure and simple?

Such a system of rank obscenity could exist only *in a world motivated by greed, where profit margin, not human dignity, is the first consideration.*

Those who say that "relative to the standards in their society, those peasants are doing *wonderfully!"* are hypocrites of the first order. They would throw a drowning man a rope, but *refuse to pull him to shore.* Then they would brag that a *rope is better than a rock.*

Rather than raising the people to true dignity, these "haves" give the world's "have-nots" just enough to make them dependent—but not enough to ever make them truly powerful. For people of true economic power have the ability to then *impact,* and not merely be subject to, "the system." And that's the last thing the creators of the system want!

So the conspiracy continues. And for most of the rich and powerful it is not a conspiracy of action, but a *conspiracy of silence.*

So go now—go your way—and by all means say *nothing* about the obscenity of a socioeconomic system which rewards a corporate executive with a 70-million-dollar bonus for increasing sales of a soft drink, while 70 million *people* can't afford the luxury of drinking the stuff—much less eating enough to stay healthy.

Don't see the obscenity of it. Call this the world's Free Market Economy, and tell everyone how *proud* you are of it.

Yet it is written:

If thou wilt be perfect,
go and sell what thou hast, and give to the poor,
and thou shalt have treasure in heaven.
But when the young man heard this, he went away,
sorrowful,
for he had great possessions.

19

I've rarely seen You so indignant. God doesn't become indignant. This proves You are not God.

God is *everything,* and God *becomes* everything. There is nothing which God is not, and all that God is experiencing of Itself, God is experiencing in, as, and through *you.* It is *your* indignation which you are feeling.

You're right. Because I agree with everything You've said.

Know that every thought I am sending you, you are receiving through the filter of your own experience, of your own truth, of your own understandings, and of your own decisions, choices, and declarations about Who You Are and Who You Choose to Be. There's no other way you can receive it. There's no other way you should.

Well, here we go again. Are You saying that none of these ideas and feelings are *Yours,* that this *whole book* could be wrong? Are You telling me that this entire experience of my conversation with You could be nothing more than a compilation of *my* thoughts and feelings on a thing?

Consider the possibility that *I am giving you* your thoughts and feelings on a thing (where do you suppose these are coming from?); that I am co-creating with you your experiences; that I am part of your decisions, choices, and declarations. Consider the possibility that I have chosen you, along with many others, to be My messenger long before this book came to be.

That's hard for me to believe.

Yes, we went over all of that in *Book 1*. Yet I will speak to this world, and I will do it, among other ways, through my teachers and my messengers. And in this book I will tell your world that its economic, political, social, and religious systems are primitive. I observe that you have the collective arrogance to think they are the best. I see the largest number of you resisting any change or improvement which takes anything away from you—never mind who it might help.

I say again, what is needed on your planet is a massive shift in consciousness. A change in your awareness. A renewed respect for all of life, and a deepened understanding of the inter-relatedness of everything.

Well, You're God. If You don't want things the way they are, why don't You change them?

As I have explained to you before, My decision from the beginning has been to give you the freedom to create your life—and hence, your Self—as you wish to *be*. You cannot know your Self as the Creator if I tell you what to create, how to create, and then force, require, or cause you to do so. If I do that, My purpose is lost.

But now, let us just notice what *has* been created on your planet, and see if it doesn't make *you* a bit indignant.

Let's look at just four inside pages of one of your major daily newspapers on a typical day.

Pick up today's paper.

Okay. It's Saturday, April 9, 1994, and I am looking at the *San Francisco Chronicle*.

Good. Open it to any page.

All right. Here's page A-7.

Fine. What do you see there?

The headline says DEVELOPING NATIONS TO DISCUSS LABOR RIGHTS.

Excellent. Go on.

The story reports on what it calls an "old schism" between industrialized nations and developing countries over labor rights. Leaders of some developing nations are said to be "fearful that a campaign to expand labor rights could create a back door means of barring their low-wage products from the rich nation's consumer markets."

It goes on to say that negotiators for Brazil, Malaysia, India, Singapore and other developing nations have refused to establish a permanent committee of the World Trade Organization which would be charged with drafting a labor rights policy.

What rights is the story talking about?

It says, "basic rights for workers," such as prohibitions on forced labor, establishment of workplace safety standards, and a guarantee of the opportunity to bargain collectively.

And why do developing nations not want such rights as part of an international agreement? I'll *tell* you why. But first, let's get clear that it's not the *workers* in those countries who resist such rights. Those "negotiators" for the developing nations are the same people, or are closely allied with the same people, *who own and run the factories.* In other words—the rich and powerful.

As in the days before the labor movement in America, those are the people now benefitting from the mass exploitation of workers.

You can be sure that they are being quietly assisted by big money in the U.S. and other rich nations, where industrialists—no longer able to unfairly exploit workers in their own nations—are subcontracting to factory owners in these developing countries (or building their own plants there) in order to exploit foreign workers who are still unprotected from being used by others to increase their already-obscene profits.

But the story says it's our government—the present administration—which is pushing for workers' rights to be part of a worldwide trade agreement.

Your current leader, Bill Clinton, is a man who believes in basic workers' rights, even if your powerful industrialists do not. He is courageously fighting big money's vested interests. Other American presidents and leaders throughout the world have been killed for less.

Are you saying President Clinton is going to be murdered?

Let's just say there are going to be tremendous powers attempting to remove him from office. They've got to get him *out* of there—just as they had to remove John Kennedy 30 years earlier.

Like Kennedy before him, Bill Clinton is doing everything big money hates. Not only pressing for workers' rights worldwide, but siding with the "little person" over the entrenched establishment on virtually every social question.

He believes it's the right of every person, for instance, to have access to adequate health care—whether or not he or she can afford to pay the exorbitant prices and fees that America's medical community has come to enjoy. He has said these costs have got to come down. That has not made him very popular with another very large segment of America's rich and powerful—from pharmaceutical manufacturers to insurance conglomerates, from medical corporations to business owners having to provide decent coverage for their workers—a great many people who are now making a lot of money are going to have to make a little bit less if America's poor are to be given universal health care.

This is not making Mr. Clinton the most popular man in town. At least not among certain elements—who have already proven in this century that they have the ability to remove a president from office.

Are you saying—?

I am saying that the struggle between the "haves" and the "have-nots" has been going on forever and is epidemic on your planet. It will ever be thus so long as economic interests, rather than humanitarian interests, run the world—so long as man's body, and not man's soul, is man's highest concern.

Well, I guess you're right. On page A-14 of the same paper there's a headline: RECESSION SPAWNS ANGER IN GERMANY. The lower headline reads, "With joblessness at postwar high, rich and poor grow further apart."

Yes. And what does this story say?

It says there is great foment among the country's laid-off engineers, professors, scientists, factory workers, carpenters, and cooks. It says the nation has encountered some economic setbacks, and there are "widespread feelings this hardship has not been fairly distributed."

That is correct. It has not been. Does the story say what has caused so many layoffs?

Yes. It says the angry employees are "workers whose employers have moved to countries where labor is cheaper."

Aha. I wonder whether many people reading your *San Francisco Chronicle* on this day saw the connection between the stories on pages A-7 and A-14.

The story also points out that when layoffs come, female workers are the first to go. It says "women comprise more than half of the jobless nationwide, and nearly two-thirds in the east."

Of course. Well, I continue to point out—though most of you do not want to see it or admit it—that your socioeconomic mechanism *systematically* discriminates against classes of people. You are *not* providing equal opportunity all the while you are loudly protesting that you *are*. You need to believe your fiction about this, though, in order to keep feeling good about yourself, and you generally resent anyone who shows you the truth. You will all deny the evidence even as it is being presented to you.

Yours is a society of ostriches.

Well—what *else* is in the newspaper on this day?

On page A-4 is a story announcing NEW FEDERAL PRESSURE TO END HOUSING BIAS. It says "Federal housing officials are putting together a plan that would force . . . the most serious efforts ever to eliminate racial discrimination in housing."

What you must ask yourself is, why must such efforts be forced?

We have a Fair Housing Act which bars discrimination in housing on the basis of race, color, religion, sex, national origin, disability, or family composition. Yet many local communities have done little to eliminate such bias. Many people in this country still feel that a person ought to be able to do what he wants to with his private property—including rent to or *not* rent to whomever he chooses.

Yet if everyone who owned rental property were allowed to make such choices, and if those choices tended to reflect a group consciousness and a generalized attitude toward certain categories and classes of people, then entire segments of the population could be systematically eliminated from any opportunity to find decent places in which to live. And, in the absence of decent *affordable housing*, land barons and slumlords would be able to charge exorbitant prices for terrible dwellings, providing little or no upkeep. And once again the rich and powerful exploit the masses, this time under the guise of "property rights."

Well, property owners should have *some* rights.

Yet when do the rights of the few infringe upon the rights of the many?

That is, and has always been, the question facing every civilized society.

Does there come a time when the higher good of all supersedes individual rights? Does society have a responsibility to itself?

Your fair housing laws are your way of saying yes.

All the failures to follow and enforce those laws are the rich and powerful's way of saying "No—all that counts are *our* rights."

Once again, your current president and his administration is forcing the issue. Not all American presidents have been so willing to confront the rich and powerful on yet another front.

I see that. The newspaper article says that Clinton Administration housing officials have initiated more investigations of housing discrimination in the brief time they've been in office *than were investigated in the prior ten years.* A spokesperson for the Fair Housing Alliance, a national advisory group in Washington, said the Clinton Administration's insistence that fair housing statutes be obeyed was something they had tried to get other administrations to do for years.

And so this current president makes even more enemies among the rich and powerful: manufacturers and industrialists, drug companies and insurance firms, doctors and medical conglomerates, and investment property owners. All people with money and influence.

As observed earlier, look for Clinton to have a tough time staying in office.

Even as this is being written—April 1994—the pressure is mounting against him.

Does your April 9, 1994, edition of the newspaper tell you anything else about the human race?

Well, back on page A-14 there's a picture of a Russian political leader brandishing his fists. Underneath the photograph is a news story headlined ZHIRINOVSKY ASSAULTS COLLEAGUES IN PARLIAMENT. The article notes that Vladimir Zhirinovsky "got into another fist fight yesterday, beating up" a political opponent and screaming in his face, "I'll have you rot in jail! I'll tear your beard out hair by hair!"

And you wonder why *nations* go to war? Here is a major leader of a massive political movement, and in the halls of Parliament he has to prove his manhood by *beating up his opponents*.

Yours is a very primitive race, where strength is all you understand. There is no true law on your planet. True Law is Natural Law—inexplicable and not *needed* to be explained or taught. It is *observable*.

True law is that law by which the people freely agree to be governed because they are governed by it, naturally. Their agreement is therefore not so much an agreement as it is a mutual recognition of what is So.

Those laws don't have to be enforced. They already *are* enforced, by the simple expedient of undeniable consequence.

Let Me give you an example. Highly evolved beings do not hit themselves on the head with a hammer, because it hurts. They also don't hit anyone *else* on the head with a hammer, for the same reason.

Evolved beings have noticed that if you hit someone else with a hammer, that person gets hurt. If you keep doing it, that person gets angry. If you keep getting him angry, he finds a hammer of his own and eventually hits you back. Evolved beings therefore know that if you hit someone else with a hammer, you are hitting yourself with a hammer. It makes no difference if you have more hammers, or a bigger hammer. Sooner or later you're going to get hurt.

This result is observable.

Now nonevolved beings—*primitive* beings—observe the same thing. They simply don't care.

Evolved beings are not willing to play "The One With The Biggest Hammer Wins." Primitive beings play nothing else.

Incidentally, this is largely a male game. Among your species, very few women are willing to play Hammers Hurt. They play a new game. They say, "If I had a hammer, I'd hammer out justice, I'd hammer out freedom, I'd hammer out love between my brothers and my sisters, all over this land."

Are you saying women are more evolved than men?

I'm making no judgment one way or the other on that. I simply observe.

You see, truth—like natural law—is observable.

Now, any law that is not natural law is not observable, and so has to be explained to you. You have to be *told* why it's for your own good. It has to be shown to you. This is not an easy task because if a thing is for your own good, *it is self-evident.*

Only that which is not self-evident has to be explained to you.

It takes a very unusual and determined person to convince people of something which is not self-evident. For this purpose you have invented politicians.

And clergy.

Scientists don't say much. They're usually not very talkative. They don't have to be. If they conduct an experiment, and it succeeds, they simply show you what they've done. The results speak for themselves. So scientists are usually quiet types, not given to verbosity. It is not necessary. The reason for their work is self-evident. Furthermore, if they try something and fail, they have nothing to say.

Not so with politicians. Even if they've *failed*, they talk. In fact, sometimes the more they fail, the more they talk.

The same is true of religions. The more they fail, the more they talk.

Yet I tell you this.

Truth and God are found in the same place: in the silence.

When you have found God, and when you have found truth, it is not necessary to talk about it. It is self-evident.

If you are *talking* a lot about God, it is probably because you are still searching. That's okay. That's all right. Just know where you are.

But teachers talk about God all the time. That's all *we* talk about in this *book*.

You teach what you choose to learn. And yes, this book does speak about Me, as well as about life, which makes this book a very good case in point. You have engaged yourself in writing this book *because you are still searching.*

Yes.

Indeed. And the same is true of those who are reading it.

But we were on the subject of creation. You asked Me at the beginning of this chapter why, if I didn't like what I was seeing on Earth, I didn't change it.

I have no judgment about what you do. I merely observe it and from time to time, as I have done in this book, describe it.

But now I must ask you—forget My observations and forget My descriptions—how do *you* feel about what you have observed of your planet's creations? You've taken just one day's stories out of the newspaper, and so far you've uncovered:

- Nations refusing to grant basic rights to workers.

- The rich getting richer and the poor getting poorer in the face of a depression in Germany.

- The government having to force property owners to obey fair housing laws in the United States.

- A powerful leader telling political opponents, "I'll have you rot in jail! I'll tear your beard out hair by hair!" while punching them in the face on the floor of the national legislature in Russia.

Anything else this newspaper has to show Me about your "civilized" society?

Well, there's a story on page A-13 headlined CIVILIANS SUFFER MOST IN ANGOLAN CIVIL WAR. The drop head says: "In rebel areas, top guns live in luxury while many thousands starve."

Enough. I'm getting the picture. And this is just one day's paper?

One *section* of one day's paper. I haven't gotten out of Section A.

And so I say again—your world's economic, political, social, and religious systems are *primitive*. I will do nothing to change that, for the reasons I've given. You must have *free choice* and *free will* in these matters in order for you to experience My highest goal for you—which is to know yourself as the Creator.

And so far, after all these thousands of years, this is how far you have evolved—this is what you have created.

Does it not make you indignant?

Yet you have done one good thing. You have come to Me for advice.

Repeatedly your "civilization" has turned to God, asking: "Where did we go wrong?" "How can we do better?" The fact that you have systematically ignored My advice on every other occasion does not stop Me from offering it again. Like a good parent, I'm always willing to offer a helpful observation when asked. Also like a good parent, I'm willing to keep loving you if I'm ignored.

So I'm describing things as they really are. And I'm telling you how you can do better. I'm doing so in a way which causes you to feel some indignation because I want to get your attention. I see that I have done so.

What could *cause* the kind of massive consciousness shift of which You've spoken now repeatedly in this book?

There is a slow chipping away happening. We are gradually stripping the block of granite which is the human experience of its unwanted excess, as a sculptor chips away to create and reveal the true beauty of the final carving.

"We"?

You and I, through our work on these books, and a great many others, messengers all. The writers, the artists, the television and movie producers. The musicians, the singers, the actors, the dancers, the teachers, the shamans, the gurus. The politicians, the leaders (yes, there are some very good ones, some very sincere ones), the doctors, the lawyers (yes, there are some very good ones,

some very sincere ones!), the moms and dads and grand-
mas and grandpas in living rooms and kitchens and back-
yards all over America, and all around the world.

You are the forbearers, the harbingers.

And the consciousness of many people is shifting.

Because of you.

Will it take a worldwide calamity, a disaster of gargantuan
proportions, as some have suggested? Must the Earth tilt on its
axis, be hit by a meteor, swallow its continents whole, before its
people will listen? Must we be visited by beings from outer
space and scared out of our minds before having sufficient sight
to realize that we are all One? Is it required that we all face the
threat of death before we can be galvanized to find a new way
to live?

Such drastic events are not necessary—but could
occur.

Will they occur?

Do you imagine that the future is predictable—even
by God? I tell you this: Your future is creatable. Create it
as you want it.

But earlier You said that in the true nature of time there *is* no
"future"; that all things are happening in the Instant Moment—
the Forever Moment of Now.

That is true.

Well, are there earthquakes and floods and meteors hitting
the planet "right now" or aren't there? Don't tell me that as
God You don't *know*.

Do you want these things to happen?

Of course not. But *You* said everything that's *going* to happen
already *has* happened—*is* happening *now*.

That is true. But the Eternal Moment of Now is also *forever changing.* It is like a mosaic—one that is always there, but constantly shifting. You can't blink, because it will be different when you open your eyes again. Watch! Look! *See?* There it goes again!

I AM CONSTANTLY CHANGING.

What makes You change?

Your idea about Me! Your *thought* about *all* of it is what makes It change—*instantly.*

Sometimes the change in the All is subtle, virtually indiscernible, depending upon the power of the thought. But when there is an intense thought—or a *collective thought*—then there is *tremendous* impact, incredible effect.

Everything changes.

So—*will* there be the kind of major, Earth-wide calamity You speak of?

I don't know. Will there?

You decide. Remember, you are choosing your reality *now.*

I choose for it not to happen.

Then it will not happen. Unless it does.

Here we go again.

Yes. You must learn to live within the contradiction. And you must understand the greatest truth: Nothing Matters.

Nothing matters?

I'll explain that in *Book 3.*

Well . . . okay, but I don't like to have to wait on these things.

There is so much here for you to absorb already. Give yourself some time. Give yourself some space.

Can we not leave yet? I sense You are leaving. You always start talking like that when You are getting ready to leave. I'd like to talk about a few other things . . . such as, for instance, beings from outer space—*are* there such things?

Actually, we were going to cover that, too, in *Book 3*.

Oh, come on, give me a glimpse, a peek.

You want to know if there is intelligent life elsewhere in the universe?
Yes. Of course.

Is it as primitive as ours?

Some of the life forms are more primitive, some less so. And some are far more advanced.

Have we been visited by such extraterrestrial beings?

Yes. Many times.

For what purpose?

To inquire. In some cases to gently assist.

How do they assist?

Oh, they give a boost now and then. For instance, surely you're aware that you've made more technological progress in the past 75 years than in *all of human history before that.*

Yes, I suppose so.

Do you imagine that everything from CAT scans to supersonic flight to computer chips you imbed in your body to regulate your heart all came from the mind of man?

Well . . . yes!

Then why didn't man think them up thousands of years before now?

I don't know. The technology wasn't available, I guess. I mean, one thing leads to another. But the beginning technology wasn't there, until it was. It's all a process of evolution.

You don't find it strange that in this billion-year process of evolution, somewhere around 75 to 100 years ago there was a huge "comprehension explosion"?

You don't see it as *outside the pattern* that many people now on the planet have seen the development of everything from radio to radar to radionics *in their lifetime?*

You don't get that what has happened here represents a quantum leap? A step forward of such magnitude and such proportion as to defy any progression of logic?

What are You saying?

I am saying, consider the possibility you've been helped.

If we're being "helped" technologically, why aren't we being helped spiritually? Why aren't we being given some assistance with this "consciousness shift"?

You are.

I am?

What do you think this book is?

Hmmm.

In addition, every day, new ideas, new thoughts, new concepts are being placed in front of you.

The process of shifting the consciousness, increasing the spiritual awareness, of an entire planet, is a slow process. It takes time and great patience. Lifetimes. Generations.

Yet slowly you are coming around. Gently you are shifting. Quietly, there is change.

And You're telling me that beings from outer space are helping us with that?

Indeed. They are among you now, many of them. They have been helping for years.

Why don't they then make themselves known? Reveal themselves? Wouldn't that render their impact twice as great?

Their purpose is to assist in the change they see that most of you desire, not create it; to foster, not force.

Were they to reveal themselves, you would be forced, by the sheer power of their presence, to accord them great honor and give their words great weight. It is preferred that the mass of people come to their own wisdom. Wisdom which comes from within is not nearly so easily discarded as wisdom which comes from another. You tend to hang on a lot longer to that which you've created than to that which you've been told.

Will we ever see them; ever come to know these extraterrestrial visitors as who they really are?

Oh, yes. The time will come when your consciousness will rise and your fear will subside, and then they will reveal themselves to you.

Some of them have already done so—with a handful of people.

What about the theory, now becoming more and more popular, that these beings are actually malevolent? Are there some who mean us harm?

Are there some human beings who mean you harm?

Yes, of course.

Some of these beings—the lesser evolved—may be judged by you in the same way. Yet remember My injunction. Judge not. No one does anything inappropriate, given one's model of the universe.

Some beings have advanced in their technology, but not in their thinking. Your race is rather like that.

But if these malevolent beings are so technologically advanced, surely they could destroy us. What's to stop them?

You are being protected.

We are?

Yes. You are being given the opportunity to live out your own destiny. Your own consciousness will create the result.

Which means?

Which means that in this, as in all things, what you think is what you get.

What you fear is what you will draw to you.

What you resist, persists.

What you look at disappears—giving you a chance to recreate it all over again, if you wish, or banish it forever from your experience.

What you choose, you experience.

Hmmm. Somehow it doesn't seem that way in my life.

Because you doubt the power. You doubt *Me*.

Probably not a good idea.

Definitely not.

20

Why do people doubt You?

Because they doubt themselves.

Why do they doubt themselves?

Because they have been told to; taught to.

By whom?

People who claimed to be representing Me.

I don't get it. Why?

Because it was a way, is the only way, to control people. You *must* doubt yourself, you see, or you would claim all your power. That would not do. That would not do at all. Not for the people who currently hold the power. They are holding the power which is yours—and they know it. And the only way to hold on to it is to stave off the world's movement toward seeing, and then solving, the two biggest problems in the human experience.

Which are?

Well, I've discussed them over and over again in this book. To summarize, then . . .

Most, if not all, of the world's problems and conflicts, and of your problems and conflicts as individuals, would be solved and resolved if you would, as a society:

1. Abandon the concept of Separation.
2. Adopt the concept of Visibility.

Never see yourself again as separate from one another, and never see yourself as separate from Me. Never tell anything but the whole truth to anyone, and never again accept anything less than *your* grandest truth about Me.

The first choice will produce the second, for when you see and understand that you are One with Everyone, you can *not* tell an untruth or withhold important data or be anything but totally visible with all others *because you will be clear that it is in your own best interests to do so.*

But this paradigm shift will take great wisdom, great courage, and massive determination. For Fear will strike at the heart of these concepts and call them false. Fear will eat at the core of these magnificent truths and make them appear hollow. Fear will distort, disdain, destroy. And so Fear will be your greatest enemy.

Yet you will not have, cannot produce, the society for which you have always yearned and of which you have always dreamed unless and until you see with wisdom and clarity the ultimate truth: that what you do to others, you do to yourself; what you fail to do for others, you fail to do for yourself; that the pain of others is your pain, and the joy of others your joy, and that when you disclaim any part of it, you disclaim a part of yourself. Now is the time to *reclaim yourself.* Now is the time to see yourself again as Who You Really Are, and thus render yourself visible again. For when you and your true relationship with God become visible, then We are *indivisible.* And nothing will ever divide Us again.

And although you will live again in the illusion of separation, using it as a tool to create your Self anew, you will henceforth move through your incarnations with enlightenment, seeing the illusion for what it is, using it playfully and joyfully to experience any aspect of Who We Are which it pleases you to experience, yet nevermore accepting it as reality. You will nevermore have to use the device of forgetfulness in order to recreate your Self anew, but will use Separation *knowingly,* simply *choosing* to manifest as That Which Is Separate for a particular reason and a particular purpose.

And when you are thus totally enlightened—that is, once more filled with the light—you may even choose, as your particular reason for returning to physical life, the re-minding of others. You may select to return to this physical life not to create and experience any new aspect of your Self, but to bring the light of truth to this place of illusion, that others may see. Then will you be a "bringer of the light." Then will you be part of The Awakening. There are others who have already done this.

They have come here to help us to know Who We Are.

Yes. They are enlightened souls, souls which have evolved. They no longer seek the next higher experience of themselves. They have already had the highest experience. They desire now only to bring news of that experience to you. They bring you the "good news." They will show you the way, and the life, of God. They will *say* "I am the way and the life. Follow me." Then they will model for you what it is like to live in the everlasting glory of conscious union with God—which is called God Consciousness.

We are always united, you and I. We cannot *not* be. It is simply impossible. Yet you live now in the unconscious experience of that unification. It is also possible to live in the physical body in conscious union with All That Is; in conscious awareness of *ultimate truth*; in conscious expression of Who You Really Are. When you do this, you serve as a model for all others, others who are living in forgetfulness. You become a living re-minder. And in this you save others from becoming permanently lost in their forgetfulness.

That *is* hell, to become lost permanently in forgetfulness. Yet I will not allow it. I will not allow a single sheep to be lost, but will send . . . a shepherd.

Indeed, many shepherds will I send, and you may choose to be one of them. And when souls are awakened by you from their slumber, re-minded once again of Who They Are, all the angels in heaven rejoice for these souls. For once they were lost, and now they are found.

There are people, holy beings, like this right now on our planet, is that not right? Not just in the past, but right now?

Yes. Always there have been. Always there will be. I will not leave you without teachers; I will not abandon the flock, but always send after it My shepherds. And there are many on your planet right now, and in other parts of the universe as well. And in some parts of the universe these beings live together in constant communion and in constant expression of the highest truth. These are the enlightened societies of which I have spoken. They exist, they are real, and they have sent you their emissaries.

You mean the Buddha, Krishna, Jesus were *spacemen?*

You said that, I didn't.

Is it true?

Is this the first time you ever heard that thought?

No, but is it *true?*

Do you believe these masters existed somewhere before they came to Earth and returned to that place after their so-called death?

Yes, I do.

And where do you suppose that place is?

I'd always thought it was what we call "heaven." I thought they came from heaven.

And where do you suppose this heaven is?

I don't know. In another realm, I guess.

Another world?

Yes . . . Oh, I see. But I would have called it *the spirit world,* not another world as we know it, not another *planet.*

It *is* the spirit world. Yet what makes you think those spirits—those Holy Spirits—cannot, or would not choose to, live elsewhere in the universe, *just as they did when they came to your world?*

I suppose I just never thought of it that way. It has not been part of my ideas about all of this.

"There are more things in heaven and earth, Horatio, than are dreamt of in your philosophy."
Your wonderful metaphysician, William Shakespeare, wrote that.

Then Jesus *was* a spaceman!

I didn't say that.

Well, *was he or wasn't he?*

Patience, My child. You jump ahead too much. There is more. So much more. We have another whole book to write.

You mean I have to wait for *Book 3?*

I told you, I promised you from the beginning. There will be three books, I said. The first would deal with individual life truths and challenges. The second would discuss truths of life as a family on this planet. And the third, I said, would cover the largest truths, having to do with the eternal questions. In this will be revealed the secrets of the universe.

Unless they are not.

Oh, man. I don't know how much more of this I can take. I mean, I'm really tired of "living in the contradiction," as You always put it. I want what's so *to be so.*

Then *so shall it be.*

Unless it's not.

That's it! That's it! You've GOT it! Now you understand the Divine Dichotomy. Now you see the whole picture. Now you comprehend *the plan.*

Everything—*everything*—that ever *was, is now, and ever will be exists right now.* And so, all that is . . . IS. Yet all that IS is constantly *changing,* for life is an *ongoing process of creation.* Therefore, in a very real sense, That Which IS . . . IS NOT.

This ISNESS is NEVER THE SAME. Which means that the ISNESS is NOT.

Well, excuse me Charlie Brown, but *good grief.* How can anything then mean anything?

It doesn't. But you are jumping ahead again! All of this in good time, My son. All of this in good time. These and other larger mysteries will all be understood after reading *Book 3.* Unless . . . all together now . . .

UNLESS THEY ARE NOT.

Precisely.

Okay, okay . . . fair enough. But between now and then—or, for that matter, for the people who may never get to read these books—what avenues can be used right here, right now, to get back to wisdom, to get back to clarity, to get back to God? Do we need to return to religion? Is that the missing link?

Return to spirituality. Forget about religion.

That statement is going to anger a lot of people.

People will react to this entire book with anger . . . unless they do not.

Why do You say, forget religion?

Because it is not good for you. Understand that in order for organized religion to succeed, it has to make people believe they *need* it. In order for people to put faith in something else, they must first lose faith in themselves. So the first task of organized religion is to make you lose faith in yourself. The second task is to make you see that *it* has the answers you do not. And the third and most important task is to make you accept its answers without question.

If you question, you start to think! If you think, you start to go back to that Source Within. Religion can't have you do that, because you're liable to come up with an answer different from what it has contrived. So religion must make you doubt your Self; must make you doubt your own ability to think straight.

The problem for religion is that very often this back-fires—for if you cannot accept without doubt your own thoughts, how can you not doubt the new ideas about God which religion has given you?

Pretty soon, you even doubt My *existence*—which, ironically, you never doubted before. When you were living by your *intuitive knowing*, you may not have had Me all figured out, but you definitely knew I was there!

It is religion which has created agnostics.

Any clear thinker who looks at what religion has done must assume religion has no God! For it is religion which has filled the hearts of men with fear of God, where once man loved That Which Is in all its splendor.

It is religion which has ordered men to bow down before God, where once man rose up in joyful outreach.

It is religion which has burdened man with worries about God's wrath, where once man sought God to *lighten* his burden!

It is religion which told man to be ashamed of his body and its most natural functions, where once man *celebrated* those functions as the greatest gifts of life!

It is religion which taught you that you must have an *intermediary* in order to reach God, where once you thought yourself to be reaching God by the simple living of your life in goodness and in truth.

And it is religion which *commanded* humans to adore God, where once humans adored God because it was impossible *not* to!

Everywhere religion has gone it has created disunity— which is the *opposite* of God.

Religion has separated man from God, man from man, man from woman—some religions actually *telling* man that he is *above* woman, even as it claims God is above man—thus setting the stage for the greatest travesties ever foisted upon half the human race.

I tell you this: God is *not* above man, and man is *not* above woman—that is *not* the "natural order of things"— but it *is* the way everyone who had power (namely, men) *wished* it was when they formed their male-worship religions, systematically editing out half the material from their final version of the "holy scriptures" and twisting the rest to fit the mold of their male model of the world.

It is religion which insists *to this very day* that women are somehow less, somehow second-class spiritual citizens, somehow not "suited" to teach the Word of God, preach the Word of God, or minister to the people.

Like children, you are still arguing over which gender is ordained by Me to be My priests!

I tell you this: You are *all* priests. *Every single one of you.*

There is no one person or class of people more "suited" to do My work than any other.

But so many of your men are just like your nations. Power hungry. They do not like to share power, merely exercise it. And they have constructed the same kind of God. A power hungry God. A God who does not like to share power but merely exercise it. Yet I tell you this: God's greatest gift is the sharing of God's power.

I would have you be like Me.

But we cannot be like You! That would be blasphemy.

The blasphemy is that you have been taught such things. I tell you this: *You have been made in the Image and Likeness of God—it is that destiny you came to fulfill.*

You did not come here to strive and to struggle and to never "get there." Nor did I send you on a mission impossible to complete.

Believe in the goodness of God, and believe in the goodness of God's creation—namely, your holy Selves.

You said something earlier in this book which intrigued me. I'd like to go back as we come to the end of this volume. You said: "Absolute Power demands absolutely nothing." Is this the nature of *God?*

You have now understood.

I have said, "God is everything, and God *becomes* everything. There is nothing which God is not, and all that God is experiencing of Itself, God is experiencing in, as, and through you." In My purest form, I am the Absolute. I am Absolutely Everything, and therefore, I need, want, and demand absolutely nothing.

From this absolutely pure form, I am as you make Me. It is as if you were finally to see God and say, "Well, what do you make of that?" Yet, no matter what you make of Me, I cannot forget, and will always return to, My Purest

Form. All the rest is a fiction. It is something you are *making up*.

There are those who would make Me a jealous God; but who could be jealous when one has, and is, Everything?

There are those who would make Me a wrathful God; but what could cause Me to be angry when I can not be hurt or damaged in any way?

There are those who would make Me a vengeful God; but on whom would I take vengeance, since all that exists is Me?

And why would I punish Myself for simply creating? Or, if you must think of us as separate, why would I create you, give *you* the power to create, give you the freedom of choice to create what you wish to experience, then punish you forever for making the "wrong" choice?

I tell you this: I would not do such a thing—and in that truth lies your freedom from the tyranny of God.

In truth, there *is* no tyranny—except in your imagination.

You may come home whenever you wish. We can be together again whenever you want. The ecstasy of your union with Me is yours to know again. At the drop of a hat. At the feel of the wind on your face. At the sound of a cricket under diamond skies on a summer night.

At the first sight of a rainbow and the first cry of a newborn babe. At the last ray of a spectacular sunset and the last breath in a spectacular life.

I am with you always, even unto the end of time. Your union with Me is complete—it always was, always is, and always will be.

You and I *are* One—both now and even forevermore.

Go now, and make of your life a statement of this truth.

Cause your days and nights to be reflections of the highest idea within you. Allow your moments of Now to be filled with the spectacular ecstasy of God made manifest through you. Do it through the expression of your Love, eternal and unconditional, for all those whose lives you touch. Be a light unto the darkness, and curse it not.

Be a bringer of the light.

You *are* that.

So be it.

In Closing

Conversations with God is all about the spiritual path of humanity. Your path, my path, and the path that our species is taking collectively.

That last part, our *collective* path, is the main focus of this, the second book in the CwG series. Here, a challenge has been placed squarely before us. This text makes it clear that the way we are "doing life" on this planet is not working. Not very well. In some cases and some places, not at all.

We should be able to do better. We have the intelligence, we have the skill, we have the technology, and we have sufficient power over our own affairs to create a world in which all of its people live together in peace and in harmony, with sufficiency and safety and serenity the hallmarks of their experience, a world in which our differences do not create divisions, our contrasts do not create conflicts, and the variations in our beliefs do not produce violence in our lives.

There is another way, yet we will not find that way by searching for it. We will find it only by creating it. And we will not create it by staying stuck in old beliefs but only by being open to new ideas, new ideas about God and about life that can truly light the world.

This book is about such new ideas. It offers a change of perspective. And this is not unimportant. This is more than a mere intellectual exercise because it is our perspective that creates our perception, our perception that creates our belief, our belief that creates our behavior, our behavior that creates our experience, and our experience that creates our reality.

It's a circle. It's the clock of eternity. And *perspective* is at twelve o'clock high.

There is only one way that I know of to change people's perspectives. You have to show them that *there is another one.* Most people think that the perspective they hold is the only way to look at things. At least, the only *reasonable* way.

I can't tell you how many folks I've talked to who have said, after hearing one of my lectures or engaging in an exchange at one of my retreats, "You know, I've never thought of it that way."

I've been struck by that.

I've never thought of it that way.

When I heard that the thousandth time, I realized that I was being given a key, a real clue here. I saw that the trick to changing the world is to get people *in* the world to think *about* the world in a new way.

That may seem obvious to you, but to me it was a revelation because all I saw all around me were individuals and organizations, all well-meaning and very dedicated, working hard to affect and to change people's *behavior,* trying to get them to *do* stuff (or *not do* stuff) rather than to think stuff.

All behaviors, I realized, spring from beliefs. No *wonder* humanity's behaviors haven't changed in millennia, no *wonder* we are still acting as barbarically as we acted in the Stone Age. Our *beliefs* haven't changed one iota. Our thoughts about most things are still the same.

Specifically, we still believe that we are separate from each other. We still believe we are separate from God. We still believe we are separate from life.

We believe that life is happening TO us, not THROUGH us.

We have no idea what's going on here. We have no idea who we really are and what our Right Relationship is to everything around us.

We see ourselves as the victims of our circumstances rather than as the creators of them.

No wonder we think there is nothing we can do!

Now if we continue to approach the challenge of altering outcomes on this planet at the level of behavior, we can cause certain behaviors in others to stop, there's no question about that. Ah, but only for a while. And *only by using force.*

Why?

Because people's behaviors spring from their innermost beliefs. Unless you do something to change their beliefs, you will have to *coerce* them to change their behaviors. You can do this, of course. You can threaten them, you can bludgeon them, you can even kill enough of them until they *give in* and do something *they don't believe in* just to stop you from hurting them.

But as soon as the hurting stops, the behaviors re-emerge because belief *always gives birth to behavior,* unless you artificially and forcefully interrupt that natural process.

On the other hand, if *belief* is what is changed, behavioral change will follow *automatically.*

Well, I looked around the world with my newfound perspective and realized that the vast, *vast* majority of organizations and individuals committed to relieving suffering and ending oppression on the planet were trying to do so at the level of *behavior.*

HARDLY ANYONE WAS DOING SO AT THE LEVEL OF BELIEF.

Wow. Feed the hungry! Clothe the poor! Free the oppressed! That's all I saw wherever I looked. But nowhere did I see a global campaign: Change Your Thinking! End Separation! Create Oneness! Unify Humanity!

And so, that has become my task. That's my self-appointed mission, my life's purpose. I've been running around everywhere doing what I can to get people to stand on a new hill, to sit in another chair, to change the place from which they are looking at things, to *alter their viewpoints.*

Or at least to get them to see that there may be *another* viewpoint, to encourage them to *just look at that,* to see if things might look differently if they would only go there and stand there on that "other hill" for just a moment. . . .

It all starts, I am clear, with our viewpoint about God. For what we believe about God, we put into place in the behaviors of humans. If we think that God loves us only under certain conditions, then we love each other only under certain conditions. If we think that God judges, condemns, and punishes, then we judge, condemn, and punish. If we think that God uses violence punitively and remedially, then we use violence punitively and remedially. We do these things with impunity, even if they are sometimes cruel, for we *use God as our Moral Authority.* What is good enough for God is good enough for us, no? How could it be otherwise?

And yet, what if our understanding of God is incomplete? What if our ideas about God are limited? What if our beliefs about God are mistaken . . . at least in part?

Could this be so?

Are we brave enough to even ask?

It was George Bernard Shaw who said, "All great truth begins as blasphemy."

He was right.

And so I go around the world "blaspheming." And now I am looking for other "blasphemers." I want to change the world's mind about God. And about life. And about each other.

I also want to help people change their minds about themselves. It is my dearest hope and my wildest dream that someday, somehow, people everywhere might see themselves, at last, as who and what they truly are: children of God (in the truest sense), individuated aspects of the Divine, with all the power and glory, magnificence, and wonder in *micro* that God is in *macro*.

A few years ago I was asked by Matt Lauer on NBC's *Today Show*, "What is God's message to the world?"

Matt said he had only thirty seconds, so urged me to keep my answer brief. I told him I could give it to him in five words.

Here is God's message to the world:

YOU'VE GOT ME ALL WRONG.

Now if that statement has no truth to it, we have nothing further to discuss. If we think we know everything there is to know about God and that, with regard to our ideas and under-standings, we've got it all *right*, then the conversation this book encourages has just ended.

The only way this conversation can continue is if we are courageous enough to acknowledge that there may be some-thing we *don't* fully understand here, the understanding of which could change everything.

I am asking you, if you think this might be true, to gather the courage to say so. To summon the strength to invite all those you know to open a new conversation on this subject. To call forth the determination to bring another idea about God into the global discussion, and to make the commitment to do all that is practical to render the message of *Conversations with God* accessible to as many people as rapidly as possible.

Why?

Because I think this message can change the world.

And I further believe that the message speaks for itself. There's very little we have to do here. We don't have to invent programs. We don't have to create organizations. We don't have to go out preaching or proselytizing. We don't have to try to convince anyone of anything. All we have to do is put this material in front of people, get it in their hands. That's it. *The material speaks for itself.* For most people, the book's impact is enormous, its wisdom is self apparent, its healing is immediate.

Every day I receive letters and e-mails from people all over the world asking me a single, plaintive question: "What can I do?"

At my public appearances I hear the same thing over and over again: "This message has changed my life. *I want to do something to give back.* I wish there was something I could do."

There is. And it is so simple.

Give a CwG book away every month.

That's it. That's all there is to it. There's nothing to join, there's nothing to attend, there's nothing to agree to or sign up for. Just . . . simply . . . *give a CwG book away every month.*

For the cost of a couple of video rentals you could change another person's life. All you have to do is join the "Reverse Book-of-the-Month Club." Instead of *receiving* a book every month, *give one away.*

If you wish to do this with a few simple mouse clicks, go to www.cwgBookShare.com. There you will find a list of all the titles in the CwG series, and you can pick the title you want to gift to another this month.

One of the things we suggest is that you do this on the same day each month. Pick a date that is meaningful to you. Perhaps it's your birthday or your favorite number. That way you'll remember. Then, on that same day each month, find a way to place a CwG book into the hands of another.

Maybe you'll send one to a friend. Maybe you'll just drop one off at the hairdresser or the doctor's office—wherever there is a waiting area with reading material. Maybe you'll "accidentally" leave a copy on the bus or the tram or the subway. You'll find a way, if you put your heart in it, to spread these books around. You'll know exactly who is "supposed" to get this month's copy!

The book I most recommend for giving away? Actually, there are two. You might wish to alternate. The first book that I find great for first-time readers is *What God Wants.* Another is *Happier Than God*. Interestingly, neither are "dialogue" books. Often, people who are new to the Conversations with God idea experience a "push back" from the notion that I have talked with God. The two books above offer wonderful introductions to the ideas in *CwG* without the reader having to embrace the "convention" of a dialogue with Deity.

However, use your own intuition on this one. If your inner voice tells you that a particular person might enjoy a different title, *go for it*. Just get out One Book a Month. Wouldn't that make a huge difference?

Yes!

Then, you may also wish to visit other pages on my personal website, particularly if you would like to stay personally connected with our work and with the energy of *Conversations with God*. Some wonderful friends and I have worked hard to make this Internet portal one of the most sophisticated and interactive New Spirituality websites in the world.

Here you will find (1) a new book, *The Holy Experience*, free for the downloading; (2) posters, podcasts, and e-cards, all for free; (3) GOD WANTS YOU TO KNOW . . . a free inspirational e-mail written by me every day and sent to your mailbox; and (4) links to other organizations supporting the placement of the CwG message into the world, including the ReCreation Foundation, Humanity's Team, and the School of the New Spirituality.

At this wonderful website you will also find The Messenger's Circle, a subscription-based *worldwide virtual CwG Community*.

Here you can (1) join the community and post a photo and whatever personal data you wish on the Profile Page; (2) ask me any question you may have regarding the CwG material; (3) hear many of my presentations of that material at RadioCWG, our audio-on-demand service; (4) participate in wonderful CwG online courses; (5) join with me in a monthly tele-class on topics straight out of the books, with some deep discussion on ways to apply those messages in every day life; (6) download a new CwG Reader every week; (7) become a Spiritual Helper in the Life Support Center; and (8) personally interact with me every day in the Reader's Forum.

I am telling you about all of this here because I want you to know that there is a whole community of people out there ready to connect with you. Many people have written me through the years telling me that they "feel so isolated" in their views about God and Life and Others, that they love the CwG material but sometimes find it difficult to connect with Like Minds. I created the CwG Community within the Messenger's Circle for just that reason. You may wish to check it out at:

http://www.nealedonaldwalsch.com/messengercircle.cfm

So do join us if you feel moved to. And whatever you decide about that, please give real consideration to our "Reverse Book-of-the-Month Club." One book a month given away by everyone reading this book right now would create a tidal wave of CwG energy in the world!

Just go to: www.cwgBookShare.com

And thanks for taking this journey through *Book 2* with me. I am excited about the possibilities for tomorrow that can emerge from our sharing this experience today.

Shall we close with a gentle thought?

> *Dear God . . . we know that you are always with us. We understand that we are not just connected with you, but One with you. We are aware that there is no separation between us. Help us now to bring that experience into our lives and into our world. Let each day and each moment be a living demonstration of this*

truth. Bring us, and all those whose lives we touch, the fullness and the richness, the wonder and the wisdom, the peace and the perfection of our True Identity, that our lives and our world may be healed. Amen and amen.

Index

Hampton Roads Publishing Company

. . . for the evolving human spirit

Hampton Roads Publishing Company
publishes books on a variety of subjects,
including spirituality, health, and other related topics.

For a copy of our latest trade catalog,
call toll-free, 800-766-8009,
or send your name and address to:

Hampton Roads Publishing Company, Inc.
1125 Stoney Ridge Road
Charlottesville, VA 22902
E-mail: hrpc@hrpub.com
Internet: www.hrpub.com